CAMBRIDGE LIBRARY COLLECTION

Books of enduring scholarly value

Women's Writing

The later twentieth century saw a huge wave of academic interest in women's writing, which led to the rediscovery of neglected works from a wide range of genres, periods and languages. Many books that were immensely popular and influential in their own day are now studied again, both for their own sake and for what they reveal about the social, political and cultural conditions of their time. A pioneering resource in this area is Orlando: Women's Writing in the British Isles from the Beginnings to the Present (http://orlando.cambridge.org), which provides entries on authors' lives and writing careers, contextual material, timelines, sets of internal links, and bibliographies. Its editors have made a major contribution to the selection of the works reissued in this series within the Cambridge Library Collection, which focuses on non-fiction publications by women on a wide range of subjects from astronomy to biography, music to political economy, and education to prison reform.

Landmarks of a Literary Life 1820-1892

Camilla Crosland (1812–95) was a British author whose literary career spanned sixty years of the nineteenth century. Although best known as a poet, she was a also a prolific writer of short stories, novels and articles. In the late 1850s she became involved with spiritualism, and published influential works on the subject. This volume, first published in 1893, contains her detailed autobiography. Crosland describes her long life chronologically, describing the aftermath of the Battle of Waterloo in 1815, the death of George III and the characters and lives of the many influential authors she met during her career. She also provides anecdotes and detailed descriptions of early Victorian society and the development of literature to appeal to a broader readership. This volume provides a fascinating retrospect of early Victorian social life. For more information on this author, see http://orlando.cambridge.org/public/svPeople?person_id=crosca

Cambridge University Press has long been a pioneer in the reissuing of out-of-print titles from its own backlist, producing digital reprints of books that are still sought after by scholars and students but could not be reprinted economically using traditional technology. The Cambridge Library Collection extends this activity to a wider range of books which are still of importance to researchers and professionals, either for the source material they contain, or as landmarks in the history of their academic discipline.

Drawing from the world-renowned collections in the Cambridge University Library, and guided by the advice of experts in each subject area, Cambridge University Press is using state-of-the-art scanning machines in its own Printing House to capture the content of each book selected for inclusion. The files are processed to give a consistently clear, crisp image, and the books finished to the high quality standard for which the Press is recognised around the world. The latest print-on-demand technology ensures that the books will remain available indefinitely, and that orders for single or multiple copies can quickly be supplied.

The Cambridge Library Collection will bring back to life books of enduring scholarly value (including out-of-copyright works originally issued by other publishers) across a wide range of disciplines in the humanities and social sciences and in science and technology.

Landmarks
of a Literary Life
1820-1892

CAMILLA CROSLAND

CAMBRIDGE
UNIVERSITY PRESS

CAMBRIDGE UNIVERSITY PRESS

Cambridge, New York, Melbourne, Madrid, Cape Town, Singapore,
São Paolo, Delhi, Dubai, Tokyo, Mexico City

Published in the United States of America by Cambridge University Press, New York

www.cambridge.org
Information on this title: www.cambridge.org/9781108021944

© in this compilation Cambridge University Press 2010

This edition first published 1893
This digitally printed version 2010

ISBN 978-1-108-02194-4 Paperback

LANDMARKS

OF

A LITERARY LIFE.

a

From a miniature painted in 1848 by Mrs Pelt.

Camilla Crosland

Sampson Low, Marston & Co Ld.   Swan Electric Engraving Co.

LANDMARKS

OF

A LITERARY LIFE

1820–1892.

BY

MRS. NEWTON CROSLAND,

(CAMILLA TOULMIN)

AUTHOR OF

"MRS. BLAKE," "HUBERT FREETH'S PROSPERITY," "THE DIAMOND WEDDING,"
"STORIES OF THE CITY OF LONDON," ETC.

" I feel like one who treads alone
Some banquet-hall deserted,
Whose lights are fled, whose garlands dead,
And all but he departed !"

THOMAS MOORE.

LONDON:

SAMPSON LOW, MARSTON & COMPANY
LIMITED,

St. Dunstan's House,

FETTER LANE, FLEET STREET, E.C.

1893.

TO THE BELOVED FRIEND,

WHOSE AFFECTION AND SYMPATHY HAVE BEEN TO ME FOR

TWENTY YEARS A SOLACE IN SORROW,

AND THE HEIGHTENER OF EVERY HAPPINESS,

TO

EDITH MILNER,

THE LOVER OF LITERATURE, AND WIELDER OF THE PEN

IN MANY DEPARTMENTS OF IT, PATRIOT AND PHILANTHROPIST,

I DEDICATE MY RECOLLECTIONS.

THOUGH BELONGING HERSELF BY BIRTH, AND ESSENTIALLY,

TO THE PALMIEST DAYS OF THE VICTORIAN ERA,

SHE EVER LOOKS BACK WITH LOVE AND REVERENCE TO

ALL THAT IS GREAT IN THE PAST,

RECOGNIZING THE JEWELS OF THOUGHT AND ACTION WHICH

THE DUST OF TIME CAN ONLY FOR A WHILE OBSCURE,

AND STRETCHES FORTH HER HANDS TO THE FUTURE, WITH

ANXIOUS HOPE AND EARNEST ENDEAVOUR TO

PLAY HER PART OF USEFULNESS WITH ENERGY AND DEVOTION.

THEREFORE IT IS THAT TO HER, AS A LINK BETWEEN

A GREAT PAST AND THE UNCERTAIN FUTURE,

I OFFER THIS LITTLE TRIBUTE AS A TOKEN OF

MY LOVE AND ADMIRATION.

CAMILLA CROSLAND.

PREFACE.

NOTWITHSTANDING the truth which underlies the French proverb, "*Qui s'excuse s'accuse*," I think it is often wise to own one's fault without waiting for the arraignment of another accuser. I find that in the following pages the personal pronoun "I" is more obtrusive than I thought it would be when, in my opening chapter, I alluded to my intention of keeping it very much in the background. These recollections have been produced under the impediments of defective sight and an afflicted right hand; consequently the handwriting was often so execrable that my dim eyes read it with difficulty, and the patience of printers must have been sorely tried. Therefore I could not give my work the prolonged personal revision which every manuscript demands from its author. Yet, on reflection, I feel how nearly impossible it would have been to relate what I had to tell without myself appearing on the scene.

Old age has its privileges as well as its penalties; four score years bring infirmities, as a matter of

course; but, were I younger, I should have had less
to relate. This seems to me the place in which to
acknowledge my obligation to Mr. Henry Johnson
for his zealous and judicious assistance in seeing my
"Landmarks" through the press; a task I should
not have dared to undertake unaided.

The composition of this book has had painful
as well as pleasant phases. It has called to mind
lost opportunities and errors of judgment, and made
me sigh anew for the "touch of a vanished hand;"
but, also, it has given me heartfelt pleasure to speak,
with knowledge, of the great and good whom it has
been my privilege to count among my friends, and,
it may be, to rescue some little facts from the verge
of that oblivion which they seemed near.

To critical readers I must bow my head; but I ask
sympathetic ones to accept my gratitude in advance,
for there is no guerdon like that of sympathy to one
who uses the pen as a means of communicating with
other minds.

C. C.

July 12th, 1893.

CONTENTS.

— ◆◇◆ —

CHAPTER I.

CHAPTER VI.

CHAPTER VII.

CHAPTER VIII.

CHAPTER IX.

CHAPTER X.

CHAPTER XI.

CHAPTER XII.

CHAPTER XIII.

CHAPTER XIV.

CHAPTER XV.

CHAPTER XVI.

LANDMARKS OF A LITERARY LIFE.

CHAPTER I.

Hearsay and childish recollections—Waterloo—Reception of the news of the battle, and anecdotes—The purser of the *Victory*—The Birmingham riots—George the Third and Queen Charlotte—Ball at Carlton House.

PROBABLY no observant person ever reaches even middle age without being conscious of those changes of manners and modes which, taking place apparently but slowly, do yet, in the course of a decade or two, bring about silent social revolutions. It is for this reason that the recollections of *any* truth-loving, truth-telling individual who has passed the allotted three-score years and ten of life, mixing in the society of a great metropolis, ought to be worth recording. Swiftly the seasons pass by; old men and women drop into their graves, taking with them memories of the past which would be precious to historians and artists; and the young spring up to mount with measured steps or rapid strides to the world's high places, or to glide into the ranks of obscure workers.

B

The young at all times have been a little too apt
to think the world was made for them, and that they,
"the heirs of all the ages," have a monopoly of
wisdom. It can never do them harm to listen to the
words of one who can recollect the scenes in which
their fathers played a part, and the times which have
made history.

It may be said that at upwards of seventy years
of age the memory becomes feeble and confused.
In my own case only in a very limited degree am
I conscious that this is true; but, because I felt
the years were passing fast away, so long back as
1865, I began making memoranda of facts, and
dates, and circumstances that appeared to me worth
noting down. So far from presuming to inflict an
autobiography on the reader, it will be my aim to
keep the obtrusive personal pronoun "I" very considerably in the background; yet I know that I
must speak of myself sometimes in connection with
scenes I shall try to describe, and must even start
with a childish recollection, though I do so to give
the reader some faith in my powers of memory.

I remember the day of the battle of Waterloo,
though, of course, only from a string of circumstances
which imprinted it on my mind. I was three years
and nine days old on that eventful Sunday, and it
happened that my father took me to spend the day
at the house of his brother, an eminent medical man,
residing in one of the suburbs of London. The

occasion afforded the first recollection I have of my cousins ; and I distinctly remember incidents of my visit, which it would be childish to relate, and in the summer twilight being lifted dead-tired on to my father's knee in the stage-coach which was to take us back to town. In my early years I was frequently reminded that *that* was the day of the battle of Waterloo.

My mother was not just then in a state of health to go so far from home; but she sat in the balcony of our house in C—— Street until past ten o'clock, watching for our return ; and now I must tell the tale as I heard her repeat it time after time.

She declared that as the light of evening faded she saw in the clouds images of horses galloping, mostly with riders, but some, she said, riderless. From her description she implied that the phantasmagoria lasted more than a quarter of an hour. Of course, when the news of the battle of Waterloo reached London the coincidence was thought extraordinary ; but so many people smiled at what they evidently supposed fancy or delusion, that, in later years, she grew cautious as to whom she related the incident. I believe, however, she learned that one or two other persons had a similar experience that evening. That it was no delusion I am certain. My mother was well endowed with common sense, had keen powers of observation, and an excellent memory, and though, like every one else, she knew that our army was on the Continent, and that a battle was expected, I believe her chief anxiety that evening was about her little girl, then her only child, who probably had never before been so many hours from under her care.

Not till the following Tuesday evening did the great news reach London. It was the night of the whist club, to which my parents belonged; and I think it was in Berners Street, at the house of Lonsdale the portrait-painter, that the friendly meeting on that occasion took place. In those days half-past four was a very common dinner-hour, and middle-class folks usually assembled to spend the evening by seven o'clock. On that eventful 20th of June the whist-players were in the full enjoyment of their games when they were startled by the newsmen's horns, and the cries of "A great victory—Buonopar*ty* defeated!" and "*Courier!*"—then considered the most authentic evening paper,—etc. I have heard the scene vividly described many times. The cards were thrown down—the gentlemen rushed into the street to procure the paper at any price the newsmen asked. The details were comparatively meagre, yet they were ample enough to convey some idea of the victory gained, and to break up the party, sending home several medical men who were present, and who intended to proceed to Brussels, or make arrangements to despatch medical students without delay. As Dr. Clutterbuck—eminent for at least another twenty years—belonged to the whist club, probably he was one of the assembly.

The ladies also departed, for their task was to be up early to look out all the old linen they could find, and set themselves to work to make lint for the wounded. Not only did surgeons from all parts of the country hasten to the scene of slaughter, but dentists had their emissaries to extract the teeth of the dead soldiers; for false teeth were then, in a grim sense, real teeth, not made of enamel. I think by nature, and still more from circumstances, I was a precocious child, and being habitually with my elders, was greatly impressed by their talk. My earliest recollections as a listener were of the talk about Waterloo; hence, every little incident in connection with it which I heard narrated took hold of my memory. Undoubtedly the writers of history have not space to give the trifling anecdotes which still vivify the scene. In my early life I knew well a lady who happened to be in Brussels that memorable June. She was then newly married, and only three and twenty years of age. So little certain of victory did the English on the spot feel, that her husband insisted on her dressing like a Normandy peasant, thinking such a costume would be a protection. Vividly have I heard her describe the partings she witnessed at the door of the hotel where she was staying, and the despair of wives who were left behind— wives soon to be widows.

Very graphically, too, did she describe the next
day's events, when women — many of whom, too
agitated to change their attire, were still elegantly
dressed—made their way somehow towards the field
of battle, returning in the army waggons, supporting
the heads of the wounded on their knees, bathing
their brows, and binding up their wounds, while a
small steady rain poured down on the faces begrimed
by powder, which yet allowed their pallor to be seen.
It is true there was no organization of lady nurses
seventy odd years ago, but I rejoice to think that
English women were capable of such heroism and
devotion years before Florence Nightingale was born.*

From Wellington and Waterloo to Nelson and
Trafalgar is not a long stride, though a retrogressive
one. I make it, partly, because, though Nelson died
nearly seven years before I was born, his deeds were
still spoken of as things of yesterday when I was
more than a little child ; but, chiefly, because Walter
Burke, the purser of the *Victory*, was one of the most

---

* I once met at a dinner-party the widow of an officer—I forget the
name—who fought at Waterloo, and the lady narrated her experience
of the "after-battle" scene. For some reason she had to cross the field
of Waterloo while it was still strewn with the dead, and for this purpose
she was blindfolded and placed on horseback, the steed being led by a
trooper. She held a handkerchief to her nose—steeped, I think she
said, with vinegar—and not until she had reached an acclivity nearly a
mile from the scene of carnage was the bandage removed from her eyes.
Then she looked back, when the field of Waterloo appeared like a field
of tombstones, for the bodies were all stripped of clothing, and shone
white in the sunshine like stones. The camp-following ghouls had
done their work effectually.

intimate and beloved friends of my parents, and from him they heard many details, not only of the life, but of the death of the hero. Walter Burke was a warm-hearted Irishman, cousin to Edmund Burke, and his portrait is to be seen at Greenwich Hospital in the picture, " The Death of Nelson." He was one of those who assisted to carry the wounded admiral down to the cockpit; and he supported him for so long a time that his arm became so thoroughly numbed that he did not recover the use of it for several hours. At the period of the battle of Trafalgar he must have been about sixty-four years of age, and is represented in the picture, which my mother saw in the artist's studio, as a little fair man, with, what used to be called, a " scratch " wig. He had three sons in the navy, and was devoted to the service. I fancy he had been several years in Nelson's ship, and spoke of many well-known events from personal knowledge. I might not, however, have introduced his name into these pages but for one circumstance.

The parentage of Horatia Nelson Thompson has been a subject of occasional discussion for more than two generations, and long ago I ranked myself among the small minority of those who did not believe the little brunette to be either the child of the blonde Lady Hamilton or of the fair-haired Nelson. Whenever the subject was broached in my mother's presence, she was invariably ready with the same remark, " Burke always said that, whoever the mother might

be, it was *not* Lady Hamilton." She always spoke as
if she thought her old friend had good reasons for his
opinion, and I doubt if any but the most absolute
evidence would have shaken her confidence in his
judgment.   Lately I have read Mr. Jefferson's clever
and laborious work on Lord Nelson and Lady Hamilton, in which the disputed question is fully treated ;
but as the author admits that some of the supposed
letters bearing on the affair were forgeries, may not
doubt be thrown on several others ?   About forty or
fifty years ago there was a perfect epidemic of forged
letters, purporting to be of celebrated persons, got up
for sale, and it is presumable that Nelson's left-hand
writing would be particularly easy to imitate.   What
sane woman would leave behind her a letter falsifying
her dying declaration ?   Mutilated in body as he was,
there was no mental decay in the " conquering hero "
of Trafalgar, not fifty years of age at the time of his
death ; and the sickly sentimentality of that particular
letter, which is supposed to establish the fact of Lady
Hamilton's relation to Nelson's adopted daughter, is
so foreign to the whole character of him whose best
beloved home was surely his quarter-deck, that the
most absolute proof is required to convince the sceptic
that the letter is genuine.   It is true that human
nature is often a bundle of contradictions, and Nelson
no doubt had his foibles.   But he was too strong a
personality not to have great leading traits.   He was
very vain, if extreme self-reliance may be so con-

sidered. He was a fighter before all things, and
ambitious beyond measure of what the world calls
glory. Probably he had not much nicer notions of
morality than most men of his age; but then he had
to the core those conventional notions of honour, which
drew a sharp line between what was considered the
excusable and the dastardly.

As for Lady Hamilton's assertion that Horatia was
Nelson's daughter, we ought to remember that she
had long resided in countries where an adopted child
is looked on in the light of legitimate offspring, and
shares legally the rights of such.

No doubt Nelson thought all was fair in war; and,
at a time when so much secret-service money was
flying about Europe, one can understand there might
be secret services that were bought in other modes
than by coin. Consider the hackney-coach story, of
which so much is made, and which rests wholly on the
hearsay statement of one who confessed she had been
suborned to do underhand work! Putting all this,
however, aside, the account was so improbable as to
be well-nigh physically impossible; and why should
Lady Hamilton have risked life and reputation when
she had her singularly flexible mother to do her
behests?

When I think of Sir William Hamilton's death—
his wife supporting him in her arms, while his hand
was clasped by Nelson's remaining one—I turn with
more and more faith to the assertion of my father's

friend, who must have had opportunities of judging
circumstances far beyond any the then unborn generations could have.   Certainly to many minds the
parentage of Nelson's adopted daughter remains as
inscrutable a mystery as the identity of the Man in
the Iron Mask, and the authorship of the Junius letters.

Whatever debt the country owed Lady Hamilton,
Nelson evidently believed it was a large one.   When
Queen Charlotte declined to receive Lady Hamilton,
the wife of our ambassador at Court, she most properly
marked her condemnation of the early immoralities of
that lovely and singularly gifted woman, nor would
that condemnation have been cancelled by the country
responding to Nelson's dying appeal.

I cannot say that I remember Mr. Burke, for he
died, I think, in 1816, but from my earliest childhood
his name was familiar to me as that of a revered
friend, for ever associated with the battle of Trafalgar.

> " From ship to ship the signal ran,
> ' England expects that every man
> This day will do his duty ! ' "

Only half an hour before the fatal shot was fired
Mr. Burke attempted to come on deck, when Nelson,
perceiving him, either repeated or pointed to the
memorable signal and exclaimed, " Go down, go
down ! Your duty is below ! "

I believe my father wrote an obituary notice of
Walter Burke for the *Morning Chronicle*, and composed a Latin epitaph for his tomb.

Perhaps, while recounting my "hearsay" recollections, I may be allowed to recall my mother's account of the Birmingham "Church and State" riots of 1791. Though not born in Birmingham, she resided there for many years of her childhood, and must have been nearly eight years old when the events occurred which made so strong an impression on her mind. She used to declare that for three days the town was virtually in the power of a wild mob, who really seemed under the delusion that they themselves were warring against anarchy. She remembered being taken by her father to the roof of their dwelling, from which at one time she beheld eleven buildings on fire, some of them being Dissenting chapels. The outbreak was provoked by a banquet given by certain radicals, then called Jacobins, in honour of the fall of the Bastille. The first proceeding of the mob, who pretended to be defending Church and State, was to break the windows of the hotel where the dinner was taking place, and then they set fire to a new meeting-house of the Dissenters. As is well known, Dr. Priestley was a great object of their wrath, and his residence was speedily sacked and destroyed. Also, they especially attacked the Quakers, of whom there were many prosperous ones in Birmingham, and the women among the rioters were seen decked in Mrs. Priestley's handsome dresses, and the delicate grey fabrics of the Quakeresses. It should be added that Mrs. Priestley was a most benevolent woman, in the habit of visiting the sick poor, accompanied by a servant who carried a basket of eatables, and often on winter evenings the "click of her pattens" was recognized when on these errands of mercy.

Of course, amid such scenes of violence there were many narrow escapes from disaster. My grandfather, being well known for a staunch Churchman and loyal subject, was personally safe, but his wife, *née* Berry, had many relatives who were Dissenters, and great anxiety was felt on their account. My mother used to tell how the courage and tact of one of them saved her house and perhaps the life of her husband. I rather think he was in hiding, at any rate he was absent from home; and when the mob demanded entrance to their dwelling his wife admitted them freely, feigned sympathy with their opinions, and entertained a number of them hospitably, not forgetting a copious supply of strong ale, so that the ruffians who came to pillage remained to carouse, departing in a state of drunken excitement, which took the turn of applauding their hostess and abstaining from the destruction they had meditated.

I wonder if it is worth while to note among "hearsay recollections," the account my mother gave of the influence of Mrs. Siddons's acting on herself when a girl of fifteen. It occasioned the only instance of somnambulism which was ever known to have occurred to her. She had been taken to see the great

actress as " Lady Macbeth," and, on the testimony of
a sister who occupied the same room, it was declared
that, though fast asleep, she rose from her bed and
went through all the action of the sleep-walking
scene. In later years my mother was so great an
admirer of John Kemble and Mrs. Siddons, that I
think she sometimes failed in doing justice to their
successors. She saw the great actors over and over
again in the same characters, with ever-renewed
pleasure, and I have heard her say that, so unvaried
was their delineation, they appeared to tread on
the very same boards of the stage each time. I
was reminded of this in reading an account of a
lecture by Mr. Irving on dramatic affairs, in which
he said something to the effect that the actor must
in the first instance surrender himself to the emotion
of his part, then conquer it, though remembering
so as to reproduce the outward expression of that
emotion.

Another of the incidents which impressed my
mother's mind as a child, but belonging to a still
earlier period, was rather a ghastly one. I have
often heard her speak of a street " peep-show," representing the execution of Louis the Sixteenth and
Marie Antoinette. Nothing so outrageous could, I
think, be permitted nowadays. The show, I believe,
was called "Guillotining of the King and Queen of
France." I suppose no events ever took such hold
of the universal English mind—and, indeed, of all

Christendom—as did the horrors of the first French Revolution.

Among my mother's lively and pleasanter recollections were some of a royal family that now may be considered historical. I mean George the Third, his queen, and their children. Before the sad circumstances which necessitated a Regency, they were often to be seen at Drury Lane or Covent Garden Theatre, enjoying the acting of Mrs. Siddons and John Kemble, or perhaps lesser luminaries, as much as the loyal audience, who were sure to evince their love and respect. In those days etiquette was very bristling, and even the ladies-in-waiting remained standing behind the royal party all the evening. I have heard my mother describe, in a somewhat too minute manner, the incessant snuff-taking of Queen Charlotte; but it was a snuff-taking age, and manners were in some respects coarser than they are at present. Far pleasanter was it to hear her expatiate on the beauty of the princesses and the evident good-nature of the king. It must be remembered that at that period and long afterwards it was only at the theatres named that what was considered the legitimate drama could be acted, the performers calling themselves "His Majesty's servants." The very few other theatres named "minor" were nearly ignored by the upper classes.

I have also often heard my mother describe a ball at Carlton House, of which, by the favour, I believe,

of an intimate old friend then in the household of the
Prince Regent, she was permitted to be a witness.
Some unseen gallery commanded a view of the
spectacle, and to this she was admitted. It was, I
believe, near the buffet, whence refreshments were
issued, and she spoke of the exquisite porcelain
cup in which she was served with tea, and the gold
teaspoon which accompanied it. This ball took
place before the Princess Charlotte was betrothed
to Prince Leopold, and just when there was talk
of a marriage for her that was most distasteful to
her. She looked grave, to a degree unnatural in a
girl in her teens, dancing chiefly, if not wholly, with
her uncles. The dress of those days must have been
about as hideous as anything which the despot fashion
ever ordained—waists ascending to the shoulder-
blades. Recalling this ball to an old friend the other
day, she reminded me that my mother used to describe the dress-coat of one of the uncles, who danced
with the princess, as being of pink satin. But the most
noticeable thing was the set of magnificent emeralds—
ill-omened gems—which the Princess Charlotte wore.

The venerable queen was seated on a throne-like
chair on a dais. She looked old and careworn, my
mother said, but "every inch a queen;" and the
Prince Regent was observed to pay the most marked
attention to her.

The rest of my hearsay and childish recollections
I must reserve for another chapter.

CHAPTER II.

Hearsay and childish recollections—French immigrants in London—
Paris in 1819—Death of George the Third.

SURELY the days of the Regency and the early
years of George the Fourth's reign—seen with the
" enchantment" which " distance lends "—form a very
suggestive period for some great novelist to treat.
In " Vanity Fair " Thackeray broke the ground, but
I think only superficially. He was a little too near
the period, and I own that to me this great work is
marred by the unchivalrous act of choosing a struggling, penniless girl, for the " villain " of his story.
There are bad women enough in the world, and it is
fit their errors and crimes should be shown up for the
edification of their sex ; but probably no class, as
a class, exemplifies nobler qualities than poor but
educated gentlewomen, who have in one way or
another to maintain themselves, and often indeed to
be the mainstay of others. For years after the
publication of " Vanity Fair " it was enough for a
struggling woman to show shrewdness and a little
more than ordinary prudence for her to be sneered

at as a Becky Sharpe. It may be that "Esmond" atones for the flaw in "Vanity Fair," but it needed as fine a work to do so.

This is a digression, I confess. I am endeavouring to depict the London life of the cultivated middle classes as I remember it to have been from my early childhood. It would indeed be gratifying if I could think that my recollections could afford hints for character-drawing to any future novelist. Certainly I think there was more individuality of character among the men than there is now—or, perhaps, it would be more correct to say eccentricity. As a rule, men were absolutely lords and masters, and little girls had to submit to the tyranny of brothers —younger brothers even—because they were boys. Of course there were radiant exceptions, and men and boys who were chivalrous by nature ; but, gene-rally speaking, every male creature set up a law for himself, to which those who were meek must submit, and which only the strong could resist. Over what red-hot ploughshares have women walked before attaining the position they now so happily hold !

In speaking of middle-class society, as it existed in London seventy or eighty years ago, one romantic element must not be forgotten, namely, the sprinkling of French refugees which moved in it. My parents were intimately acquainted with the Gautherot family, the members of which I knew exceedingly well. Madame Gautherot, the first wife of M. Gautherot, had been

C

sub-governess in the Orleans family under Madame
de Genlis ; and the Gautherots, I understood, fled to
England in the days of the Terror. He, I believe,
had held some musical appointment about the French
Court. He had, however, long been married to his
English wife in the days I am describing ; and what
a blessing was that active, sensible, practical manager
in a family of brain-workers! She was always called
" Mrs.," not " Madame," and as the generality of
people gave the *th* in Gautherot the English sound,
her name did not seem very French. She was not,
I fancy, much older than the two elder daughters, who
were, respectively, professors of the harp and piano,
and had their annual concert, usually at the house of
some lady of rank. The harp-player gave lessons to
the Princess Charlotte even after her marriage, I suppose, for I remember hearing anecdotes of the royal
pair at Claremont. The Mademoiselles Gautherot
were thorough, high-bred gentlewomen, and liked the
observance of proper etiquette. Though nearly my
mother's own age, they sometimes asked her to be
their chaperon, as was the case when they witnessed
the *début* of Madame Vestris from the pit of Her
Majesty's Theatre in 1815. The *débutante* was said
to be only sixteen, but was in reality eighteen, her
age having been ascertained many years later in order
to decide a bet on the subject.

M. Gautherot dwells in my mind as quite a typical
Frenchman of the period. His daughters—there was

a younger one whom I only vaguely recollect—spoke
English perfectly, but he, though so long a resident in
London, scarcely understood a word of the language
that must have always been buzzing about him. He,
too, was a professor of music. I best remember his
violoncello, but rather think he taught several in-
struments. The family occupied a good house in
Nassau Street, one of those old-fashioned London
houses that are more roomy than they look. The
drawing-room, with its lounges and easy-chairs of
white and gold, was a very elegant apartment; its
appointments being years in advance of the furniture
usually seen in similar dwellings.

I think the Gautherots must have been most
kindly people, though the father was never reconciled
to his exile. On one occasion the harpist sent her
harp to our house, adding a charm to a little
evening party by her playing. I dare say she had
often done so before, but I remember the special
occasion because I—at six or seven years old—was
naughty enough to steal into the drawing-room the
next morning before the harp was taken away that I
might try to play on it.

Only as a scene by daylight do I recollect the
Nassau Street house, when I accompanied my mother
in a morning visit. In those days it was the custom
to offer morning visitors cake and wine; but, instead,
our French friends gave us delicious milled chocolate
—Spanish chocolate, I think it was called—having a

white froth at the top of the tiny china cup in which
it was served.   I have never since tasted anything
comparable with it.   On one afternoon I recollect
that M. Gautherot was at home ; it must have been
winter-time, for daylight was fading.   There was
talk of my being about to commence music, when the
old man beckoned me to him, and, stretching forth
his long, thin, brownish fingers, volunteered to teach
me the lines and spaces of the treble clef by them.   I
learnt my lesson of *f, a, c, e,* etc., by the fingers, and
spaces between them in a few moments, though one
of the daughters was interpreter on the occasion.

My parents used to spend pleasant evenings sometimes in Nassau Street, where they often met interesting people—emigrants, always charged with anecdotes
of poor Marie Antoinette and her husband, not one
of them, probably, believing that the Dauphin could
have lived long.   From what I have heard, and what
I remember, the presence of the French refugees in
London must have had a very beneficial influence in
society.   They were almost always well educated,
with much more of all-round culture than the English
of that period often attained ; and they were tem-
perate in an age when nearly all men were more or
less wine-bibbers.   They must have been astonish-
ingly economical and thrifty to have lived as they
did.   As all the world knows, there were members of
the old noblesse, all their previous lives accustomed
to ease and luxury, who turned their acquirements to

practical account ; and, while they taught their own
language, often painting and music as well, and even
dancing, in our middle-class families, they insensibly
left a leaven of refinement behind them which was
not quite unneeded. Of course every rude schoolboy believed that one Englishman was a match for
three Frenchmen ; and I fear the emigrants must
sometimes have felt themselves despised. But they
lived down bitterness, and were always grateful to
the English friends who treated them with consideration. Many returned to France before Waterloo, but
also many, like the Gautherots, had formed English
ties, and must have left descendants who are now
thoroughly loyal British subjects. When we remember how many of our eminent people have
claimed descent from the old Huguenot stock, we
cannot but feel how near of kin we are to the great
French nation.

Old fashion-prints will show how hideous was the
dress in England when this century was still in its
teens. The waists were so short that the buttons on
men's coats and the termination of a woman's bodice
were literally between the shoulder-blades. Frock-
coats were unknown, and the universal swallow-tails
were often of bright blue with brass buttons.
Women's skirts were absurdly scanty and short—too
tight, I fancy, for a pocket to be conveniently used ;
hence, I suppose, the introduction of the reticule
—often a very handsome little bag, carried on the

arm, or suspended on the corner of the chair in use. I think the uneasy chairs of those days always had corners. But the bad taste of the dress was a small affair compared to the fact that few women wore sufficiently warm winter clothing. Multitudes of people never wore any wool near the skin; and even when snow was on the ground little girls shivered in low frocks and short sleeves. I remember my little black frock made for mourning for the Princess Charlotte, with its edging of white round the short sleeves; and I know, in the winter, I was always sorry when the after-dinner time came that my pinafore must be removed, because, thin as it was, it afforded some little warmth. I was a delicate child, kept very much in warm rooms, and accustomed to a bedroom fire; but every tender care must, I think, have been somewhat neutralized by the unseasonable dress.

It was *à propos* of a later fashion, when boys were the victims, that I heard an eminent medical man declare that thousands of children were killed every year in the attempt to make them little Highlanders. Of course, when ladies' dresses scarcely reached to their ankles, great attention was paid to their *chaussure;* but thick shoes and warm stockings would have been terribly " hoofish ; " so only silk stockings, or very fine cotton, with thin-soled and sandal-tied shoes, were worn, often even in the streets.

The long war with France and the general diffi-

culty of intercourse with the Continent had thrown
England very much on her own resources in matters
of taste; and it must be owned she had not shone
under the ordeal. I remember two or three very
old ladies who preserved something of the old-school
style, and still wore powder, and I think never
adopted the very short waist; but dress with the
younger generation was hideous. The usual furniture was also formal and tasteless. It may be
admitted that we have gone to the other extreme,
and overcrowd our rooms with knickknacks. But
in my childhood a French or Swiss clock on the
chimney-piece—which most probably did not go,
since it was said no English clockmaker could repair
a foreign timepiece—was the chief ornament of a
drawing-room, neighboured, however, by a pair of
lustres to hold candles and a few oddments of china.
A workbox and a writing-desk on some side-table
might be seen, and a looking-glass and a few pictures,
probably. But, when the room was arranged, the
straight-back chairs were placed formally against the
walls. A sofa there would most likely be, with a
sofa-table before it—that is, a table with flaps, which,
when extended, made the table the length of the
sofa—but seldom would an easy-chair be seen. In
the dining-room of middle-class families horse-hair
chairs, with two armchairs among them, were very
common. But a thick Turkey carpet would comfort
the feet, and the dining-table would shine like a

mirror ; for those were the days when the cloth was removed for dessert, and the decanters of wine glided round in baized stands so as not to scratch the mahogany.

I think there was a very genuine love of flowers in those times, though they were much less lavishly used than now, and were less varied, and less in the nature of exotics. London balconies were often crowded with hardy plants, and boxes of mignonette were much in vogue. In fact, when furniture for the most part was square and ugly, wall-papers hideous, and good pictures not abundant, flowers were often the only refining influence of the house. And, alas ! there was one form of ugliness pervading all classes, of which the present generation can with difficulty form an idea.

If the ill-informed and dangerous fanatics who preach against vaccination could only behold the countenances, marred almost out of resemblance to the human face divine, which were common every-where seventy years ago, surely they would hide their own faces in shame. I really think that, of the men and women born before 1780, fully half were more or less marked by the ravages of small-pox. From that date inoculation became more general ; but sometimes the disease was malignant even after inoculation, and, if it did not kill, left disfiguring traces behind. Besides, it served to propagate the disease. I can call to mind several elderly people, so seamed and scarred, that they almost frightened me when a child. Certainly for sixty years I have seen nothing comparable to the cicatrized faces so common in my childhood. Ladies, so afflicted, habitually wore the thickest of veils out of doors, and probably chose the darkest corners when in society.

But, if a dangerous and loathsome illness, followed by lifelong disfigurement, was a calamity, what shall we say to the total blindness which, in disastrous cases, was sometimes the result?

It would be difficult to exaggerate the horrors, which Jenner's discovery so greatly lightened, if it did not wholly banish. Readers of eighteenth-century fiction must have noticed how often an attack of small-pox is made the *Deus ex machina* to curb vanity, test constancy, or break off a marriage —a sure sign of its deadly power. In fact, a girl who had gone through an attack without retaining its fatal signs was considered " beautiful for ever," and probably, in many cases, gave herself airs accordingly.

It was said that the lady to whom the first Duke of Wellington was engaged before he went to India had her beauty marred by the fatal disease in his absence ; that, like a true woman, she, on her re-covery, wrote to release him from his engagement ; but that he, like a true and chivalrous knight, refused to be released, and the lady became his duchess and the mother of his sons.

There is one more hearsay reminiscence which may be worth giving before I close this chapter of recollections of my very early childhood. Though, when the Continent was opened to tourists after the final overthrow of Napoleon, only a very limited number of English people had visited Paris up to the period of 1819, yet, in the summer of that year, my parents spent nearly a fortnight there under peculiar circumstances. A client of my father's, who owed him between three and four thousand pounds —a large portion of it either advanced in the prosecution of a lawsuit, or to be considered as liabilities incurred from having become a security—had fled to France, when the Continent seemed secure, setting his creditors at defiance. He had a rich wife, with a fortune settled on herself, and his eldest son had married an heiress. Thus the family were able to live luxuriously abroad. Subsequently one of the daughters married into the Thellusson family. Negotiations had always been going on with the hope of some business settlement, and, I fancy, comparatively small sums had been remitted to England. In the summer of 1819 Mr. G—— proposed to meet my father at Dover on a certain day to have a conference on his affairs; and, either for a summer jaunt, or more likely because he wished for my mother's presence at the meeting, he took her with him. When they reached Dover they found, instead of the personage expected, a letter, enclosing a twenty-pound note to pay the expenses of the journey, and entreating my father to come on to Paris and be his guest ; and on they both went.

Of course my mother had not made any toilet preparations commensurate with such a journey and such a visit; yet, under the circumstances, I do not think she winced much at the ordeal before her. But after the passage across the silver streak and the tedious *diligence* journey, which she was wont piteously to describe, she reached Paris, and was indeed astonished at the mode which prevailed. French fashions were not then followed as swiftly as they now are. English women were still wearing short waists, and petticoats reaching only to the ankles, while Parisians had skirts nearly touching the ground, and waists almost where they ought to be. Of course my mother felt herself an object; but the ladies of the G—— family set about mending matters as well as they could. At their suggestion, and with the needful help to unpick and alter, skirts were dropped to the shoes, and the waist lengthened by sashes several inches broad. I still remember those beautiful ribbons, the most beautiful I had ever then seen. There were several of these sashes, which no doubt gave sufficient variety of costume to my mother's white dresses.

To such guests such hosts would naturally be very affable, and I have heard my mother speak feelingly of the evident pain and humiliation the grown-up daughters felt at their father's position. Of course the sight-seeing that could be experienced in ten or twelve days was gone through, and I have heard my mother expatiate on the narrow dirty streets, without side pavement, with the feeble light of the oil lamps, suspended in the middle—and which enabled her to realize what was meant by the revolutionary cry of *à la lanterne.* In one of the churches—I think it was Notre Dame—she saw the Duchesse d'Angoulême, and described her as looking like a woman who had never smiled. Alas! for the daughter of Marie Antoinette and Louis Seize! But chiefly do I record this visit of my parents to Paris because they spoke of the Buonapartist feeling which so evidently prevailed, especially among the humbler classes. Of course the English were well hated; and yet the driver of the *diligence,* on the return journey to England, talked freely to my father of the prevailing sentiment, and took from his pocket a fan which, when closed, showed a portrait of Louis Dix-huit, but when opened represented Napoleon and the little king of Rome.

Of course my father and mother brought home a few mementos of their visit to Paris, one of which, a reticule, chiefly composed of minute garnets, I still possess. And I remember an ingenious toy, unrivalled in England for many years, and a receptacle for *bonbons,* covered with bright blue satin, of the tint in Paris called Marie Louise, but which in England had long been known as Waterloo blue. My father might have brought home a trifle of money, but I fear he was chiefly laden with promises never to be fulfilled.

A few months later—one cold January evening— I was bidden to listen to the tolling of the great bell of St. Paul's, for it announced that "the poor old king" was dead. I think that, as yet, George the Third as man and king is scarcely appreciated. Those who look deepest into his reign will, I am persuaded, feel that in a number of instances he played well a very difficult part. I think Carlyle's sneer about Robert Burns being set to gauge ale-barrels while George the Third had to steer through a French revolution, an American war, and Manchester riots, unworthy of that great writer. Had George the Third been born a peasant and set to gauge ale-barrels, we may be very sure he would have done his work dutifully; but Robert Burns could no more have acted well a kingly part than his Sovereign could have written "The Cotter's Saturday Night."

I remember with what deep affection "the poor old king," as in his affliction he was commonly called, was usually spoken of by those who remembered his earlier years; and the description of him in his last days, current at the time of his death, made a life-long impression on my childish imagination. A blind old man with a white beard, that reached to his waist, beguiling the dreariness of a blue-walled, padded chamber, by playing Handel's music on a pianoforte—or harpsichord, I forget which—until the keys were hollowed by his fingers.

Thus began the memorable year 1820. It closed for me with the death of my dear father in December —a death that, after a few days' illness, altered all the prospects of his family, completely dwarfed the plans that had been formed for my education and advancement, and filled my mind prematurely with worldly cares and anxieties.

I believe I shall have few more hearsay recollections to narrate, but rather my own personal recollections of people and events that in many instances can now be remembered by only a few survivors.

CHAPTER III.

Coronation of George the Fourth—And recollections of his reign.

MY father—like Mrs. Charles Kemble, as her daughter
records—"hated a fool," and I should imagine, from
various circumstances, had no horror of a really
learned lady. At any rate, he had planned for my
education that it should have the solid foundation of
Latin and Greek. But his death, when I was eight
and a half years old, resulted in long years of
straitened circumstances; and the teaching at a good
day school was all my mother could afford me.
Thus, with a very brief exception, to be measured by
weeks rather than months, when I was placed with
an excellent teacher, I was, out of school hours,
nearly always in the society of my elders. I
mention this, and one or two other personal circumstances, to account for my taking an interest
in events which surely must have been little heeded
by the generality of children. I had a younger
brother—a high-spirited and thoroughly boyish boy,
of whom by-and-by I shall have to speak in connection with an historical event; but, whatever his

merits, he was little of a companion to his quiet, book-loving sister; so that in many respects I was lifted prematurely out of childish thoughts and childish interests.

But my mother had been my father's second wife; and I had two half-brothers, the elder of whom died in India, after distinguishing himself in various ways. He was the first to introduce gas to the streets of Calcutta. The younger, thirteen years older than I, had studied for the law; but the disastrous loss my father had experienced through Mr. G—— had delayed the articling of my brother H., so that, though probably as well instructed as if the necessary formalities had been gone through, he was not able at once to take up my father's connection. He was, however, very promptly articled to a solicitor, with an understanding that he was to benefit by the business he could retain. This dear brother seemed henceforth half father as well as brother to me. I had always been his pet and plaything; and the tie of affection between us was always most sweet. Burthened as he was with the responsibility of doing all that he possibly could for my mother and her children, I think there is little wonder that, even after becoming an admitted solicitor, he was not a very successful one from a monetary point of view. He had a fine taste for literature, music, and art, but was not exactly of the stuff of which famous lawyers are made. There was too much that was feminine in his nature for so severe a profession ; feminine, not effeminate, for on occasion he could be brave as a lion. At a period when tenderness for animals was rather ridiculed than otherwise, he cared not for laughter if the cat perched on his shoulder.

H. taught me many things, and, above all, chess, when I was about ten years old, of which I tell, because it affords me the opportunity of saying my say in favour of teaching the game to children. I am persuaded the cultivation of chess as a recreation in childhood gives the mind a spring; and years after I first played I remember hearing of Dr. C——, a schoolmaster at Hammersmith, who encouraged his boys to play chess on Sunday. Whether Dr. C—— was a D.D. or an LL.D., I know not ; but I think he was a wise man, and that his boys, in the few otherwise idle hours of Sunday, were better employed than if they had filled up the time according to their own sweet will.

The first public event of the "twenties" which I distinctly recollect was the coronation of George the Fourth, which took place in July, 1821. Of course the champion business, the backing horse, and the gauntlet of defiance were what impressed my childish imagination most, and served to imprint other details on my mind. My parents were intimately acquainted with Monsieur V——, whose position at Carlton House was officially called "Clerk of the Kitchen," whatever that may mean. He was a man of active

D

benevolence, but a little retiring and shy, as if
conscious of speaking English too indifferently to
enjoy English society. But, in fact, his duties were
so absorbing that he seldom mixed in it. When his
wife entertained friends at their apartments in St.
James's Palace, he perhaps dropped in for half an
hour, and that was all. She was a Scotch woman, of
more than average culture, a woman who thought as
well as read. She was an ardent admirer of Pope;
and, from her quotations and recitations from his
translation of Homer, did I first form any idea of
the "Iliad."

The preparations for the coronation banquet de-
volved on Monsieur V——, and I understood that for
the three weeks previous to it he never went to bed.
The day before the occasion, assistance was found to
run short, and I believe many gentlemen, "for the
fun of the thing," donned the garb of waiters and
officiated in that capacity. I always understood that
my brother might have been one of these had he so
pleased. The coronation ceremonies were said to
have been a great fatigue to the elderly and prematurely worn-out monarch. Six sisters, the Misses
W——, one of whom I afterwards knew, strewed
flowers before the king as he walked in procession.

I wonder if any reader will sympathise with my
feeling about flowers, and agree with me that their
spirit-breath bears a divine message, and that it is
meet that they should neither be trampled under-

foot, even by the most exalted of human beings,
nor thrown into a grave with the dead !

The attempt of the unhappy, unfortunate, and ill-
advised Queen Caroline to force her way into the
Abbey is now matter of history ; but well I remember
the talk of the time about her. I think people are
often sadly careless as to what they say in the presence of children on subjects which the young cannot
possibly understand. They think that the un-under-
stood passes from the mind unheeded, whereas the
observant child often ponders and ruminates, and
ends by falling into some absurd opinion. Partisan
spirit ran very high on the subject of Queen
Caroline's trial ; and one day I was asked by a little
girl, younger than myself, neither of us being ten
years old, whether I was " for the king or the queen."
I promptly answered, " For the queen," and she as
promptly retorted, " Oh, we are for the king." I had
heard the queen very much pitied, and I believe the
chief idea I grasped was that it was very cruel not
to let her adopt a little boy if she wished to do so. I
fancy there are few people now who do not consider
she was worthy of pity. The circumstances of her
marriage were horrible ; her worst faults, those of
wrong-headedness and imprudence, were the result
of a very imperfect education ; conceding that, she
did not endure the scorn and contumely with which
she was treated with the resignation of a saint.

A little incident, of which my mother was an eye-witness, illustrated the want of tact and forbearance on the part of poor Queen Caroline which often increased her troubles. It chanced that the king— it might have been when he was only Prince Regent —and his discarded wife were at the same theatre the same evening, their respective boxes being on the opposite sides of the house. After the loyal greeting of the audience had been acknowledged by the king and he had taken his seat, Queen Caroline rose, and from the front of her box made him a stately courtesy; in return the king rose and bowed to her with equal formality. Surely it would have been wiser of her to have shrouded herself behind the curtain of her box!

A few weeks after the coronation of her husband, Caroline of Brunswick passed away, and I was taken to see her unostentatious funeral *cortége* pass along the New Road. The day was one of those chilly, rainy summer days which are so depressing; and people commented on the weather being in harmony with the occasion.

I have alluded to M. V——, who occupied apartments in St. James's Palace. A somewhat humorous incident occurs to me, in which the Clerk of the Kitchen showed himself fully equal to an emergency.

One day the king—I think it was when he was Prince Regent—sent for Monsieur V——, wishing to speak to him. "Amand," he exclaimed, addressing him by his Christian name, always with George the

Fourth a mark of favour, "I have been told that to
enjoy a beefsteak in perfection it should be eaten
direct from the gridiron, so I am thinking of bringing
a friend or two to sup off one in the kitchen." No
doubt the conversation was in French, though I
heard it reported in English. I think the scene
was at Carlton House, the following evening being
the one appointed. The proposed supper was certainly a "new departure." Short as the time was for
preparation, Monsieur V—— was able to have the
kitchen hung with crimson cloth and otherwise deco-
rated, until it appeared a handsome *salle à manger ;*
only the grilling took place in the presence of the
prince and his boon-companions. What other viands
were added to the homely steak I know not; but
the supper was pronounced a great success, and the
revelry of it lasted for hours, Monsieur V—— being
warmly complimented on his achievement.

I wonder if the literary men who some time in the
"fifties" established the "kitchen club," periodically
excluding their servants from the lower regions to
practise or witness culinary operations, were aware
that they had been partially forestalled by so fine a
gentleman and rare an epicure as George the Fourth!

I wish I could describe the London of the days
of George the Fourth as vividly as it remains in
my own memory. I beheld Regent Street in the
process of building, and when the southern portion
of it was a mass of scaffolding. I recollect when one

end of St. Martin's Lane must have occupied the site
of Trafalgar Square, for it led to a narrow part of the
Strand where one had to crane the neck to look up
at the lion on Northumberland House. London is
now a city of palaces—then it was a picturesque old
place that must have been delightful to a cultivated
antiquary, so rich was it in historical associations.
Even in childhood it was a great pleasure to me to
have the scene of a famous event pointed out to me,
or to be instructed in the customs of a preceding age.
I remember one or two sedan chairs waiting for hire
near the West End squares ; but they were worn and
shabby, though with likeness enough of their better
selves to recall Hogarth's pictures to mind.   In
keeping with the sedan chairs were the huge ex-
tinguishers remaining at the doors of many good
houses, and used to put out the torches that were
required when oil-lamps were feeble and gas was
as yet undreamed of. Small as London was, compared with its present magnitude, I have no recollection of the thoroughfares being crowded as they are
nowadays.   But very noisy the streets were when
the roadways were composed of great stones, the
macadamizing process only coming in, I think, with
the "twenties." Not that the noise proceeded from
excess of vehicular traffic, for cabs were not introduced until about 1826, and omnibuses not till two
or three years later.

There were, however, hackney coaches in abun-

dance, large lumbering vehicles that at a pinch were
capable of holding six persons. These coaches—
with, usually, old men for drivers, and drawn by a
pair of sorry-looking steeds—were generally the discarded carriages of the nobility and gentry, and had
no doubt seen long service in rural districts and on
bad roads before they sank to their humbler condition. But even in their decay the thick cushions
and faded linings of these hackney coaches told of
better days, and seemed out of harmony with the
musty straw at the bottom. A gentleman of the old
school, who died a nonagenarian, used to declare that
in the last century the best glass for carriage windows
was made by a person living in Smithfield, who died
without revealing the secret of the manufacture ; and
that so highly were his wares esteemed for their
transparency, that when hackney coaches were dis-
continued, opticians eagerly bought up such old glass
of this fine quality as remained in connection with
them, for the purpose of grinding into eyeglasses and
spectacles.

I may mention that in the days of George the
Fourth the Haymarket justified its name ; for at
least once a week, and I think oftener, the top of it
was well-nigh blocked up by the fragrant loads of
hay which often reached to the first floor windows of
the houses, the carts remaining stationary for hours,
with their shafts resting on the ground, after the
horses had been removed. It was, in fact, the regular

hay-market, and in breezy weather particles of hay
were blown about in all directions. It must have
been about the time when omnibuses began to run
that the hay-carts ceased to obstruct a busy thorough-
fare.

There was a celebrity of the eighteenth century,
whom I well remember, as he appeared in the early
days of George the Fourth's reign—an old man of, I
should think, more than eighty years of age. This
was Major Cartwright, a man who, in comparatively
early life, had voluntarily sacrificed his worldly prospects. An officer in the British navy, already somewhat distinguished, he withdrew from the service
rather than fight against the Americans, with whom
he sympathized in their declaration of independence.
A fine proceeding this seemed in the eyes of certain
shallow thinkers who made a hero of him, but perhaps
the world would be more of a bedlam and battle-field
even than it is if our sailors and soldiers usurped the
authority of their rulers instead of obeying them.

Shortly after his retirement from the navy, Major
Cartwright received a commission as major in the
Nottinghamshire Militia, hence the title by which
he was subsequently known. For some years he
was our near neighbour, a tall, thin, venerable-looking
old man, with that bleached complexion which is
often seen at an advanced period of life, but which has
nothing sickly about it. I think he could never have
gone out in other than very genial weather, for he

dwells in my memory as attired in summer clothing, nankeen "tights," with gaiters, and a long, flapped waistcoat. I never saw him walking alone; for generally he had a friend on each side, with whom he seemed to be enjoying conversation. But as, with sauntering pace, he passed some houses from which he was recognized, the exclamations inside were, "Horrid Radical," "Shocking Republican," etc., for the sight of him was as a "red rag" to provoke the ire of the Tories. Yet now there is a statue of Major Cartwright in Burton Crescent, his place of residence for years, and erected after his death by sympathizing admirers. Be it understood that, in the early "twenties," Burton Crescent was a locality in high repute as the residence of wealthy merchants and professional men. The garden was kept in exquisite order, each householder having a key, and in those ante-police days the "beadle," who seemed constantly on the watch, was the terror of naughty children if they attempted to pluck flowers, or break down the shrubs.

In those early days of George the Fourth's reign, and indeed while my friend lived, I knew well a stockbroker of some eminence, who used to tell an amusing story of the great Rothschild, as the founder of the English branch of the family used to be called. Mr. D. H—— was also of the "chosen people," and like some others of his "nation," whom I have been fortunate enough to know, a man of marked integrity and active benevolence.   When he was a very young man he often transacted affairs with Rothschild, but on one occasion the business on the exchange which he had to transact was on so small a scale that he took it to a less famous house.   Somehow or other Rothschild heard that he had done so, and, the next time they met, rebuked him by asking why he had not come to him.

"Oh, sir," replied Mr. D. H——, "I thought a matter of eighteenpence too small to bring here."

"Ah, but bishness is bishness," returned the great man.

My old friend described the scene in a lively manner, and said that Mrs. Rothschild was generally at the counting-house, keeping the books, and wearing two watches, according to an ostentatious though short-lived fashion, when women displayed their watches at the waist.

I remember a silhouette of the great Rothschild, a form of portraiture very common at the beginning of this century.   It represented a large man of very rotund figure.   Mentioning these black profiles reminds me of a Frenchman who, in the "twenties," dispensed with the usual silhouette machinery, but cut out admirable likenesses with a pair of scissors by merely looking at his subject.   He had been an officer in the "grand army" under the first Napoleon.

CHAPTER IV.

Mrs. Davison and her son, the future musical critic of the *Times*—A glimpse of Miss O'Neill, Miss S. Booth, and an anecdote of the "Young Roscius"—Edmund Kean—Charles Kemble—Malibran.

A MORE interesting person, to me, however, than Major Cartwright, or even the great Rothschild, was the well-known actress, Mrs. Davison—the Miss Duncan who for many years held sway as the exponent of what was called "genteel comedy." She was our near neighbour, and my mother and she were great friends, while her two sons were the playmates of my younger brother E. ; my playmates, or, at any rate, child-companions, also, I might say, for they were not boisterous boys. The elder, James, became the celebrated musical critic of the *Times*, and I recollect the old five and a half octaves piano, on which—not till he was advanced in his teens—he first learned to play. As all who knew him must remember, he was lame, a misfortune which was the consequence of an accident in infancy, his nurse having let him fall, and concealed an injury that he received until too late to repair it.

I confess to having some faith in what is called a

desultory education. I believe it often suits genius remarkably well. I cannot say I remember distinctly the details of the education of the two Davisons— they seemed to be often at home, and perhaps for a portion of their boyhood only attended a day school. But I do well recollect that James was a devourer of books, even at eleven or twelve years of age. If one called at the house, and "Jem" was at home, it was pretty certain that he would be found reading; if one met him in the street he always seemed to have a book under his arm, or probably several volumes held together by a strap; for the Davisons had a friend in a neighbouring street who possessed a fine library, and I understood that the boys were allowed the free use of it. In those days circulating libraries were poor affairs, never supplying readers with history, biography, or any works of real educational value; and intelligent young people of both sexes were often largely indebted to the generosity of kind lenders. Perhaps now that there are so many methods of obtaining books, undreamed of in the "twenties," there is some excuse for the people who decline to lend their books—and there are two sides to the question. I think no one should hinder the sale of a good book by offering to lend it; though the loan may be a priceless boon to one who is too poor to otherwise procure the coveted treasure. There was something really beautiful in the brotherly love of the two boys, the younger, without a spice of jealousy, recognizing in childhood the ability and attainments of the elder. There could have been only a year or two of difference in age between them, and they were slightly my juniors, but I remember how William appealed to his brother, or if James were not present, he would certainly find occasion to say, "I must ask Jem," or "Jem thinks," or "I must tell Jem," showing how one mind leaned on the other. Not that William was deficient in mental ability, far otherwise ; and I think he must have had, what phrenologists call, constructiveness to a large degree, for he excelled in making toy coaches, etc., out of pasteboard, painting and finishing them to perfection.

In private life Mrs. Davison was an admirable woman ; and she was a fine actress of that old school which, to the general public of to-day, can be but a tradition. Of course her prime was past when I knew her, and I never saw her personate any of the youthful characters by the sustaining of which she had gained eminence ; but I recollect her when engaged at the Haymarket, I think about 1824, playing important but rather matronly parts—often in conjunction with Liston, when she well sustained her high reputation, and was greeted with warm applause by the old playgoers. It was about this time, or a little earlier, that she was somewhat hurt by being "cast" by the manager for "Mrs. Candour" in the *School for Scandal;* but the revenge she took was to act this subordinate part so well that it was said she played down the "Lady Teazle." She had a fine figure, and fine features, which, being a little pronounced, made her look handsomer on the stage than off; but the charm of her acting was its natural-ness. Her enunciation was distinct, and the dialogue from her lips seemed the easy flow of conversation, whether the scene were vivacious or pathetic.

Like so many great actors, Mrs. Davison was on the stage early, and she used to tell the story of Miss Farren, who married the Earl of Derby, throwing her hoop over the young girl in the green-room, saying, "You will be the Lady Teazle after me!" a predic-tion which was fulfilled, for that character was one in which she became famous. By the way, I wonder if any great actor will arise to represent "Sir Peter Teazle" as the man of fifty, as Sheridan describes him, and not the senile septuagenarian that is generally por-trayed! Undoubtedly he is the only true gentleman in that very clever but most unpleasant play, and deserves better treatment than he meets. Mrs. Davison's character in *The Rivals* was "Maria," which some people used to say was a more important one than "Lydia Languish;" and in an edition of *The Rivals* which I once saw, a portrait of Miss Duncan as "Maria" was the frontispiece. My recol-lection of her kindly gracious manners is still keen, and I can imagine how great an actress she must have been in her youth.

There was another actress of not less celebrity than
Mrs. Davison of whom I must say a few words.
This was Sarah Booth, who, about the period of my
birth, brought a letter of introduction to my parents
from some one in the north of England. She was
then a young girl of nineteen or twenty, who had
already made a high reputation in the provinces, but
came to London to commence a five years' engagement at Covent Garden as a leading actress. She
had a great success as "Juliet," and there is a full-
length portrait of her in the potion scene, now trans-
ferred to the Dramatic College. But I saw it frequently when it hung on the staircase in the house
she occupied for many years in Bloomsbury Square
The likeness was excellent, but the dress—white
satin, I think—was in the short-waisted style of the
day. For when Miss S. Booth, as she was always
called in the playbills, personated "Juliet," small
attention was paid to fitness of costume, and mediæval
heroines were commonly dressed in a modern style.

Sarah Booth was a well-informed and thorough
gentlewoman ; the youngest of three sisters and the
support of her family, including a widowed mother
and a young brother, until, through her influence, a
Government appointment was procured for the latter.
Her talents were versatile, for, though the personation
of "Juliet" was one of her triumphs, she played in
comedy with equal success. She had often taken the
heroines' parts in conjunction with Betty, the boy-

actor, who was called the "Young Roscius," and declared that though apparently inspired on the stage, he was still the child off it. She said that often behind the scenes she played marbles with him between the acts, a game of which he seemed never to tire. My elders used to speak with genuine regret of the falling off there was when young Betty reappeared in manhood, only showing himself as a very mediocre performer. Miss Booth was quite the leading actress of her theatre until Miss O'Neill appeared and took the town by storm. I believe it was in 1817 that Sarah Booth's five years' engagement expired, and, though the managers desired to engage her for another term of five years, she refused to be considered second to Miss O'Neill, and accepted a lucrative engagement in Dublin. It was shortly before she left London that a little incident occurred which I believe, in no slight degree, influenced my life.

I should mention that I was so early a playgoer that I have no recollection of there being any novelty in my going to the theatres. Probably our intimacy with Sarah Booth, who often sent us orders, was the occasion of these—wise or unwise—indulgences. I fear they were injurious to health, but not mentally hurtful, I am very sure.

One evening Miss Booth had been dining at our house—a five-o'clock dinner I think it was—with the understanding that she must leave early, as she had to deliver an epilogue after the tragedy in which Miss

O'Neill was performing. She had promised to take
my mother with her to the theatre ; and, to my great
delight, I was allowed to go with them. I fancy I had
been put to sleep on the sofa for two or three hours
previously, or could hardly have been so wide awake,
as I certainly was, when lifted into the hackney-coach
at between nine and ten o'clock at night, for I could
have been little more than five years old when
the circumstance took place. To this day I
remember vividly the incidents of that evening—the
being ushered into Miss Booth's dressing-room, a
spacious apartment, where a bright fire blazed, and
where at each end a toilet-table was arranged with
tall wax candles lighted. The second toilet-table
was reserved for another actress of some celebrity—
Mrs. Egerton, I think—but whom I did not see.
There was an air of luxurious comfort about the room
which impressed me, and the door was shielded by
the first *portière* I can recollect seeing.

I stood by Miss Booth while she dabbed her cheeks
with rouge, a process which I did not think improved
her. Soon there was a knock at the door, and the
portière was lifted by a tall gentlemanly man, who
presently seemed to be a particularly kind one. I
think he must have been a man who liked children,
and with whom, consequently, children are at ease.
I fancy my mother was anxious that I should be
able to say I had seen Miss O'Neill. The tragedy
in which she was acting was not quite over. I

E

remember being in charge of the tall gentleman,
who talked to me, and, I suppose, listened to my
chatter. At the stage door he tossed me up on
to his left arm, just as a nurse tosses up a much
younger child, in order that my eyes might be on a
level with a broad slit in the door. Through this
slit not only the stage but the whole house was
visible. What I saw on the stage was a figure in
white, making gestures which, of course, I could not
comprehend, and uttering language I did not understand. Neither did I comprehend the epilogue, which,
after the green curtain had fallen, Miss Booth came
forward to deliver in just the same dress she had worn
all the evening, a thing that seemed strange. But
what impressed me was the crowded pit, the sea of
upturned faces which it presented, nearly all masculine, with a very large proportion of bald heads. I
fancy few women were found to attempt the crush
that was encountered in the struggle for a seat in the
pit in the days of Miss O'Neill, when people waited
in the street, with more or less patience, for hours
before the doors opened. Young as I was the scene
made a life-long impression. When, in the early days
of my womanhood, it became painfully apparent that
I must "earn my own living," it was with inclination
amounting to desire, that my thoughts turned to the
stage, identifying myself with some of Shakespeare's
heroines. I even dreamed vividly several times of
being about to appear on the stage, but ever there

came before me the scene of those upturned faces, which I felt I never could encounter. Often I regretted my weakness ; yet I have learned to believe, that when, throughout life, our wills and wishes are overmastered by some apparently trivial incident or recollection, the overmastering is by a Divine Hand, and for our benefit. Worldly prosperity is not the highest good which that Hand has to bestow. I know that childish recollection was revivified a multitude of times, no doubt for a wise purpose, for in my subsequent playgoing I hardly ever looked at the white and gold stage doors, customary in theatres, without wondering what eyes were gazing through their slits, and recalling a scene which even now, after more than seventy years, is as fresh as ever.

For the first half of my life I was a frequent playgoer, and may be allowed to recall some of the recollections of my early youth. I must have been about seventeen or eighteen years of age when my dear brother H. took me to see the elder Kean as "Shylock" and "Othello." It may be a sort of heresy, but I believe the young, supposing they are imaginative and impressionable, are not the worst judges of acting. Unspoilt by the cant of criticism, their hearts are touched by every stroke of true genius, without their reasoning on the why or wherefore they are affected. I dare say Edmund Kean was an uncertain actor, but at his best he was assuredly supreme. I can fancy a commonplace actor would represent "Shylock" as fiendish, but Edmund Kean made the Jew human—a man torn by revenge for many injuries, and especially heart-wrung by the desertion of his daughter for a Christian. In the scene where he hears of "Jessica's" proceedings, and how she had bartered for a monkey the ring she had stolen, "Shylock" exclaims: "Thou torturest me, Tubal! It was my turquoise; I had it of Leah, when I was a bachelor. I would not have given it for a wilderness of monkeys." I can never forget the depth of anguish he expressed in these few words—anguish that was hardly mastered by his revenge throughout his magnificent personation of "Shylock." My impression of Edmund Kean is that he could express the extremes of tragic emotion, yet without crossing the boundary-line which separates it from extravagance and bombast. I think he was more of a momentarily inspired actor than the patient accomplished artist.

The "Portia" on the occasion referred to was Miss Philips, a young actress whom I had previously seen in Miss Mitford's play of *Rienzi*. I think she had only been a year or two on the stage when she married and retired into private life, but she deserves a word of recognition. Tall, graceful, and dignified, she seemed to me an ideal "Portia."

Twice I saw Edmund Kean in *Othello*, and I imagine his representation of the "Moor" was as grand an achievement as was ever witnessed on the stage. I do not think *Othello* is a woman's play, and I still like it the least of what are called Shakespeare's five greatest dramas. "Desdemona" is a poor creature that calls forth no loftier feeling than pity; and groundless jealousy is not a quality that women feel inclined to condone. But Kean made the famous soldier, the happy "Othello," so tender and true that the heart went out to him to the bitter end. In *Othello* there are several very effective speeches, and I especially remember the one that ends with the line—

"Farewell! Othello's occupation's gone."

There seemed tears, a strong man's unshed tears, in the voice, and the effect on the audience was electric. There was the hush of rapt attention while the words were delivered, a few seconds of absolute silence, and then the simultaneous thunderburst of applause!

We were in about the third row of the pit—of Drury Lane Theatre, I think it was—and in those days when stalls were not, a good seat in the pit was unquestionably the best place in the house. Middle-class families were generally great playgoers, and—unless they took benefit tickets for some favourite—seldom went elsewhere. Habitual frequenters of the pit knew a "dodge" or two by which a good seat could generally be secured. I only remember one drawback. Bonnets were bonnets in those days, and ladies were pretty sure to be requested by some one behind them to take off their bonnets, which hindered a view of the stage. This seemed a nuisance, but had to be done, for bonnets were large sheltering headgear at this period. Admission to the pit was three-and-sixpence at Drury Lane and Covent Garden, and only at these theatres, and at what was called the little theatre in the Haymarket, could the drama styled "legitimate" be acted. Actors always said if they satisfied the pit—if the pit "rose to them" was a phrase used— all must be going well.

Those three-and-sixpences—multiplied by three or four—rolled out of the pocket of pater pretty often in many a circle of what is now called the upper middle-class. Pieces were not so elaborately set on the stage, consequently there was more variety in the bills; and even when a new play was having a run it was often only acted three times a week, so that there were changes for alternate nights.

I suppose that according to the modern code of opinions it is heretical to hint that the sumptuous elaboration of scenery and dress may be carried too far! Yet, personally, I feel that the admiration elicited from an audience by the ultra-realistic setting up of a play distracts the attention from the play itself. It is a trite saying that actors and managers live to please, and must please to live. Of latter years it has seemed, in my humble opinion, that

they have set themselves to please mainly the
pleasure-loving throng instead of the select few,
whose far-reaching approval would in the long run
elevate the taste of the many. Fifty or sixty years
ago parents took their sons and daughters to see a
fine play less as an amusement than that they might
benefit by its influence on their minds. I am afraid
Shakespeare, though more talked about, is less
studied now than then. Of course there are glorious
exceptions ; but, as a rule, I fear authors and actors,
and every description of artists, are less sensitive to
the duties of their high calling, less conscious of the
responsibility entailed by the talents confided to
them, than once upon a time they were. Periods
there have been when the painter was the sublime
exponent of human emotions and Divine lessons,
and when the stage, obeying " Hamlet's " instructions,
" held, as 'twere, the mirror up to Nature, showed
Virtue her own feature, Scorn her own image, and the
very age and body of the Time his form and pressure."
But now the painter too often thinks first of subjects
that will please the many—that is, the mediocre class
—and, consequently, tell ; and the dramatist and
actor seek before all things to amuse the masses,
indifferent apparently to the task of elevating them.
Also, people run after one favourite performer,
comparatively indifferent to the manner in which
the subordinate characters are represented. It was
not so when Charles Kemble acted " Cassio," or

"Faulconbridge," or "Mercutio;" or, a little later on, when Keeley's "Peter," in *Romeo and Juliet*, became a personage that "brought down" the house. By-the-by, why is "Juliet's" foster-nurse always represented as an old woman? Shakespeare could not have intended her to be more than seven or eight and thirty. Possibly there might be a very effective rendering of her as a woman in the prime of life, a plebeian tolerated as the close associate of he young mistress from the office she had filled, ignorant, garrulous, unscrupulous, with just as much touch of vulgarity as one dare to associate with an Italian.

I shall not presume to write of actors, whose triumphs are still remembered by thousands of the general public; but Malibran must have been dead more than fifty years, and I desire to chronicle my opinion that she was one of the greatest actresses that ever lived. Her singing was delicious; but of that I will not speak. Her acting in the *Sonnambula* was in its way as powerful as anything I remember of the elder Kean's. How she sang, if it were only recitative, and at the same time expressed in gesture and movement the passion of the opera, was something marvellous. Especially does memory recall the scene with "Elvino," in which she asserts her innocence to her unbelieving lover. Kneeling to him, he repulsing her, she clinging to his ankle, till he dragged her quite across the Drury Lane stage, her loosened hair streaming and touching

the ground. This description seems suggestive only
of the exaggeration which oversteps the limits of
high histrionic art. But the reality did not. One
night a voice near us in the pit—that of a man
apparently approaching forty years of age, exclaimed
audibly, "My G—, how can he stand it!" There
was a story widely believed, though perhaps only
ben trovato, that after some impassioned scene,
probably the one I have described, Malibran once
seized a pot of porter belonging to a stage carpenter
and refreshed herself with a draught, and that ever
afterwards the beverage was provided for her. But
another anecdote I had from one of her intimates.
It was that stage dresses were trouble enough to
Malibran, without having to think of the ordinary
shifting fashions for private life; so she paid a
West End milliner a hundred a year to keep her well
dressed through all the varying seasons, without the
fuss and worry of choosing for herself. An eminently
wise arrangement, it seems to me, supposing the
wearer and provider of the dresses could rely on
according taste.

CHAPTER V.

The British Legion in Spain—Education for women—The old reading-
room of the British Museum—Accession of Queen Victoria.

THE seven years' reign of William the Fourth was in
many respects a very eventful one. The discussion
concerning, and the passing of the Reform Bill, caused
an agitation in every grade of society, of which it
must be very difficult for the present generation to
form any idea. Optimists and pessimists, elderly
and middle-aged, swang their pendulums to the
extreme of their opinions. On one side we were told
to expect universal prosperity, on the other that the
country was going to destruction. I think the result
was that the generality of young men, as well as
young women, instead of taking a patriotic and
enlightened interest in public affairs, as they might
have done under different circumstances, grew heartily
tired of politics. Not that my contemporaries were
altogether frivolous, for the "Tracts for the Times"
stirred up deep feelings and led to ample discussion.
But undoubtedly it was at this time that the pleasure-
loving era among the masses set in. Cabs and

omnibuses were well established, and made "getting about" easy. Places of entertainment multiplied, as well as newspapers and cheap and amusing literature. Old people were in a measure dazed by the rapid changes that were going on, and greatly relaxed their control over the young, though of course there were a few grand exceptions that served as clogs to the wheels rolling on somewhat dangerously.

One of the noteworthy events of the Sailor King's reign was the enrolment of the British Legion to serve in Spain to uphold the rights of the infant Queen Isabella, under the regency of her mother, whose name they adopted, calling themselves Christinos. My younger brother E., who was at this time (1835) in his twentieth year, had always desired to be a soldier,—his wish being something far more earnest than the short-lived fancy so many boys entertain. He really never took interest in any reading but stories of adventure. Tall, well made, good looking, and with perfect health, and utterly fearless, he was of the very stuff of which good soldiers are made ; but in our circumstances it was impossible to gratify his inclinations. He had been in one or two situations that were entirely distasteful to him, and one day, without any preliminary warning, announced to my mother that he had enlisted as a private—under a false name—in the British Legion, then on the point of sailing for Santander. It appeared that he

had formed the acquaintance of a Major Younghusband, who held a commission in the Legion, and
who had assured him that if he would take this step
he would certainly be raised from the ranks, and have
a commission given him soon after landing in Spain.
We were dismayed at what E. had done, but there
was no help for it, since he would not have drawn
back, even had he been aided to do so. It would
appear that Major Younghusband had really taken
a liking for my brother, but he died a few weeks
after the troops sailed, and E. found himself
without the one friend on whom he had relied, and
with comrades who were, for the most part, desperate
characters, with whom he could have but little fellow-
ship. Nevertheless, the brief tidings we had from
him were more cheerful than the circumstances really
warranted. Yet this was to be expected from a
high-spirited youth, who had wilfully chosen his lot.
But a time came when many weeks passed without
a letter. In those days news was not flashed daily
from one country to another, and the newspaper
accounts of the British Legion were meagre and far
between. At last we received a short letter, evidently
written under difficulties, stating that E., with a large
proportion of the troop to which he belonged, had
been stricken with fever, and imploring that a little
money might be sent to procure the food so necessary
for a convalescent. When the banknote which was
forwarded reached him, he still lay on his wretched

bed, with many others, in a barn-like building which had been converted into a hospital, unable to use his money until he had an opportunity of enlisting the services of the doctor, who took charge of it, spending it slowly and discreetly in milk and other necessaries, so as not to attract attention; for, as my brother subsequently said, he was surrounded by men who would have murdered him had they known there were a few pounds under his pillow.

As time went on we were extremely anxious, until one day I received a letter or message, I forget which, from my dear uncle, George Toulmin, begging me to come to him as soon as possible, for a very urgent reason. Uncle George was a bachelor, a retired naval officer, with very little income besides his half-pay; but he was one of the kindest, most affectionate, and generous of mortals, and among his several nephews I am inclined to think E. was his favourite. Our Uncle George had never tied himself down to a permanent home, but liked the independence of living in lodgings, which he could change at a short notice, and pass from town to the seaside, or take a trip to the Continent at his own pleasure. At the time of which I am telling he occupied rooms on the outskirts of town, and when, in obedience to his summons, I presented myself, he met me in the hall. There was the usual cordial greeting, but more than customary gravity in his face, and perhaps I said, "What is it?" for the first

words I remember his uttering were, "E. is here!"
I saw the parlour door was open, and instinctively,
with an exclamation of surprise, moved quickly
towards it, but my uncle in a measure stayed me
and prepared me for a shock.

Never shall I forget the object which presented
itself. No stage get-up could, I think, quite imitate
my poor brother's appearance. Gaunt and thin, and
pale with a yellow paleness, quite foreign to his
naturally clear healthy complexion, with faded,
stained regimentals that looked as if the sleeves and
legs had never been quite long enough for him, he
seemed the very type of the poor, weather-beaten
soldier. Of course I sprang towards him, but he
moved back a little, exclaiming, "Don't touch me,
I'm covered with vermin!"

It was a terrible story of misery and semi-starvation
he had to tell. Whose fault it was that the leaders
of the detachment to which my brother belonged
were unprovided with funds I am not prepared to
say; but his account was that, almost from the
moment of landing in Spain, the privations of the
troops began. He declared that sometimes they
were twenty-four hours without food, and that when
it arrived the animals were living. Oxen were hastily
slaughtered, and their flesh, not half cooked, was
devoured by the famishing men. Being untrained
recruits, harassing drill had to be endured, and all
sorts of hardships encountered. No wonder fever

broke out among them, something, I imagine, like the jail fever of which we read, produced by bad and insufficient food, dirt, and overcrowding. Numbers died, and the wonder seems rather that any survived. So miserable was the attendance on the sick, that E. declared that for five weeks not even his face was washed. Some of the horrors he witnessed he described to my mother, but not at the time did she give me an idea of their nature. I suppose the authorities were glad to be rid of a number of useless invalids, and a party, of which my brother was one— an entire detachment, I think—was shipped back to England, on the condition, he said, of signing a receipt for the pay they had never received! The threadbare uniform in which my brother stood was all the clothing he had with him. It was thoughtful of him not to present himself to his mother in the plight in which I beheld him, and generous of our kind uncle to shelter him. Of course, a few hours sufficed to re-establish him among us, and it was surprising how speedily wholesome living, acting on youth and a magnificent constitution, restored him to health, though perhaps he never quite recovered his early vigour. Subsequently he went to India in a mercantile capacity, formed a partnership with another young Englishman, a cousin of Martin Tupper's, as an up-country trader —still seeking a life of adventure—but died before he was thirty years of age.

I have said that in the reign of William the Fourth the pleasure-loving era among the masses set in ; but among what is now called the upper middle-class a change of opinion was brooding which has had momentous results.   In the early "thirties" there still lingered a strong objection to a gentlewoman, if unblessed with fortune, maintaining herself even by tuition ; and becoming a governess, although of a very high grade, was thought to compromise her position in society.   I grieve to think that something of the same feeling still prevails, but it is weak and evanescent compared with the rank prejudice which then existed.   If a woman possessed literary ability she might write books and so obtain money, but there was a by-law which made her understand that she did so at the risk of being ridiculed and despised by the other sex.   I recollect that in 1833 a purchase was made at a charity bazaar of two little sealed packets labelled respectively, "A Lady's Horror" and "a Gentleman's Horror."   They only contained the shape of a stocking, one cut in black paper and called "A Black Leg," and the other in blue inscribed "A Blue Stocking."

One other pursuit there was sometimes open to the class I have named, but which was only a degree less compromising than being a governess, and this was portrait-painting, usually miniature painting on ivory.   This lovely art, now nearly superseded by photography, had one cruel drawback, for a few years' practice of it usually ruined the sight, if it did not produce ultimate blindness.

Of course, when there were so few openings for impoverished gentlewomen, a different tone of feeling prevailed among male relatives from that which exists at the present day. They did not altogether admire independence of character in women, and felt, for the most part, that there would be shame in brothers, or even more distant relatives, allowing the sister or niece to fight the battle of life unarmed for the conflict, as they considered her to be.

Personally, I have never belonged to, or much admired, what is called, the "shrieking sisterhood," yet I confess that we weaker women owe much to their untiring struggles and vehement protests. Portionless girls of the present day cannot, I think, easily realize the condition of women similarly circumstanced at the time of which I am telling. They were in the swaddling-clothes of ignorant prejudice, which there was seldom a hand ready to loosen. Accomplishments were thought all in all, especially music, which was often quite neglected after marriage ; and a girl's reading was generally so circumscribed that she had small chance of mental development, unless the home library were far more extensive than that which was usually found in a middle-class family. In those days lending libraries seldom supplied anything beyond new novels, and though some of these have survived to become classics, a mental

F

diet composed wholly of fiction, however excellent, is not nourishing.

I think it was Professor Craik who said in one of his essays that with women the pursuit of knowledge was always "under difficulties." And I am very sure that when he wrote, and in the long ago that I remember, it was literally true. Of course there were a few, but I fear a very few, grand exceptions; but, as a rule, when girls had left school they were thought to be wasting time if seen reading. They were allowed to spend their superfluous energy in fancy work, and ridiculous wax-flower making, without molestation; but "put down your book," and "don't waste your time that way," were common expressions. I do not say this was the case in my own home, but I witnessed it where I visited.

Yet the very parents who grudged their girls the mental development of a book, thought it no waste of time for them to spend two or three hours a day at the piano. Of course it is rank heresy to breathe a word against music, the youngest of the arts, but the least thought-inspiring—music that "soothes the savage breast," etc.; but it does seem to me that the cultivation of music is one of those things which should be kept within due limits. Where there is great natural ability, aid its development if you will, but to warp the mind away from nobler studies for the sake of cultivating music is often a cruelty. Unless music, which always appeals to the feelings, is consecrated to the highest services, or fully balanced by severer studies, it may have a very enervating influence. Some little proficiency in it is often made the excuse for many mental deficiencies and for indulgence in frivolous pleasures. Indeed the fruits of over-cultivation of music are now apparent. Our housemaids take sixpenny lessons on the piano, and think themselves "young ladies," on the strength of playing a 'few tunes badly, and singing love-lorn ditties; and music halls are acknowledged to have too often a demoralizing influence. Music is very seductive, it is apt to beguile the mind from sterner occupations, and has the refrain of "Fly not yet" about it in the haunts of pleasure. It may be that the national character wants invigorating rather than "soothing," and if mean music were less cultivated, perhaps the influence of the higher soul-inspiring sort might more prevail.

My dear brother H. died in 1838; and it was a year or two after that event that I became a reader at the British Museum. I should like to describe the old reading-room as it was in those days. The entrance was by a very unpretending gateway in Montagu Place, a street leading out of Russell Square. It was a long room, with a slight odour of Russian leather, as massive volumes were arranged all round, many of which must have been bound in that delightful style. A sort of counter at the end of the room separated it from a portion of the vast library, which

could be seen at intervals when any of the officials
lifted the curtain hung across an opening behind the
counter. On each side of the room were large
leather-covered tables with substantial reading-desks,
and inkstands well filled with always limpid ink, and
delightful quill pens of a very large size, were provided, as well as comfortable chairs. So few were
the readers, that though each table might have
accommodated three or four persons, even if each
had a heap of books before him, I think it was
only on one occasion that I failed to have a table
to myself. Lady readers were so much in the
minority that I do not remember ever seeing more
than two or three besides myself. Perhaps it was
this minority which rendered the officials so obliging
to us. Especially I call to mind one gentleman,
named Marshall, I was told, who was the Keeper
of the Manuscripts. He was often of the greatest
service to me. From the books for which I asked,
he must have judged that I was reading up for
some special object, and when he found what that
object was, he put me on the track by mentioning
works of which I had never heard. He must have
been wonderfully erudite, for I believe he did the
same for many other readers. He seemed to know
instinctively where any particular information was to
be gained. Often "my table" was loaded with more
books than I could consult in the day, and then he
would kindly inquire which I would like put away for

my next visit, without my incurring the delay of a fresh looking out. There was some convenient receptacle under the counter into which he put them. Among the books into which I dived was a certain folio Holinshed, remarkable from the fact that some Shakespearian student had underlined the numerous passages to which the great dramatist had been indebted in several of his historical plays. Quite wonderful was it to observe how often the mere transposition of a word converted the graphic prose of the old writer into Shakespeare's sonorous blank verse. Long paragraphs were there, replete with phrases that are household words from the plays in which we are accustomed to find them.

Alas! after a month or two's devotion to the Museum, I had to give up my self-appointed task, finding that it would occupy years properly to accomplish, instead of the few months which alone I could have devoted to it. But those days spent in the old reading-room are pleasant spots in my memory. The steady, sufficient, but not glaring light—the silence only broken by an occasional whisper or the sound of the little waggons that brought in heavy books, made it conducive to earnest study ; and, indeed, I think only real students used the national library in those days.

Some years later I had occasion a few times to visit a new reading-room—not the present one, which I have never seen—and I confess the contrast jarred upon me. It was a great room that seemed garish, from the blazing sunshine which pervaded almost every corner. There were many tables, most of them crowded, but some of the readers lounged, in a manner I had never seen in the old room—and many were restless, and looked tired from standing over the great catalogues. There was no substitute for the courteous Mr. Marshall; and the subordinate officials seemed harassed and overworked. There were plenty of lady readers by 1850. I suppose there are people "fearfully and wonderfully made," who can think in a strong sunlight; but, for myself, I now understood what was meant by a "Museum headache," and when I had obtained the historical information I was then seeking, I took my leave of the reading-room with a dim foreshadowing that it would be for ever.

I may mention an incident which occurred in 1841, and which impressed itself on my mind, probably because it had cognate bearing on the subject for which I was reading in my earliest visits to the Museum. I met, several times in society, a lineal descendant of a brother of Jane Lane, the heroine who assisted Charles the Second in his escape after the battle of Worcester, and heard from his lips some details which are not recorded in any of the histories of the period with which I have met, and perhaps may be new to some of my readers.

It is well known that the fugitive king was dis-
guised as a servant, and that Mistress Jane Lane
rode on a pillion behind him, acting her part so well
that his identity was unsuspected. But Mr. Lane
told me that at the end of the long and perilous ride
the king asked his companion what he could do to
requite the service she had rendered him.

" Let us use (or quarter) the Royal Arms," she
promptly replied.

" Nay," returned Charles, " I cannot do that ; but
you shall assume a portion of them."

I am not sure which was the word mentioned, " use "
or " quarter," but after telling me of the above incident,
Mr. Lane gave me an impression from the seal he
was wearing. Unfortunately, in the course of time,
the wax got crushed and broken ; but I am nearly
sure that the portion of the Royal Arms assumed
consisted of the three lions on the sinister side of
the shield ; and I distinctly remember that the crest
was a horse's head and fore legs, with the hoofs
holding a crown, the motto being *Garde le Roi.*
Jane Lane was a single woman, of about eight or
nine and twenty, at the time of the battle of Worcester,
though she married subsequently. No doubt books
of heraldry give the Lane arms, though probably
without mentioning their origin.*

* When I saw that Jane Lane was to be included in the " Dictionary
of National Biography," I sent these particulars to the editors of that
work. My communication was politely acknowledged, though whether
it afforded information not already possessed I do not know.

Assuredly the most memorable event of the "thirties" was the accession of our beloved Queen. Of course the nation had watched the career of the young princess, though without much knowledge of the privacy of her life. And yet there was an instinctive admiration for her mother, the Duchess of Kent, and the wise manner in which she had guarded and guided the heiress-presumptive to the throne. Little anecdotes of the thoughtful kindness of the young princess did ooze out, and if sometimes they were only *ben trovato*, they had their value for all that; since a *ben trovato* anecdote of a distinguished personage generally only mirrors a truth. "On ne prête qu'aux riches," said a shrewd Frenchman.

Little did I think when I first heard the Queen prayed for on Sunday, June 25, 1837, that I should live to witness her glorious jubilee, and lay before her the tribute which I am tempted to reproduce here.

> We, who in years long fled remember well
>   Her youthful maiden bloom and rose-crowned brow,
>   Where regal jewels early learned to glow,
> Claim as a right the choral song to swell
> Of jubilant thanksgiving !   There doth dwell
>   In Memory's hallowed chambers a great show
>   Of trials past, of glory and of woe
> Borne royally, as England's records tell.
> The reaper Death has mowed our ranks among
>   Until we are but few ; and it may be
> Our voices scarce are heard amid the throng
>   Of younger minstrels piping full of glee,
> Yet our *Te Deum* mingles with the song,
>   Its solemn notes that ring of memory !

We, who can recollect the child Princess
   So full of promise, amply justified,
   Are stirr'd more deeply as the long years glide,
Though we but murmur low " May God Her bless,
And spare Her for Her people's happiness,"
   Than those still sailing upon Life's flood-tide
   Whose clarion notes proclaim their love and pride
From shore to shore with hearty eagerness.
Victoria ! writ large in lines of light,
   The name through coming ages will remain
In foremost rank with those great few, that blight
   Ne'er tarnished, shining on without a stain ;
A victor warrior fighting " the good fight,"
   'Mid perils and temptations for our gain.

CHAPTER VI.

The brothers Chambers—The "forties"—"Delta"—The
sister of Burns.

IT was in the spring of 1841 that I first addressed
Messrs. Chambers of Edinburgh, sending them a
prose article and a poem, which were promptly inserted in their *Journal;* and very soon I had the
pleasure of feeling myself an acceptable contributor.
When the brothers came to London they called upon
me, introducing me to their wives, and what began
in a purely business acquaintanceship soon ripened
into a warm and lifelong friendship.   Seldom, I
think, have two brothers done so much good in the
world as the brothers William and Robert Chambers ;
and it is because I knew them so well and for so
long a period, that I feel justified in writing about
them at some length.

In the year 1845 I spent nearly two months in
Scotland, being a guest in either one family or the
other the whole time ; but I already knew my hosts
intimately from having seen them frequently in
London, and thus at once felt I was visiting friends.

Still what is called "staying with people" makes us more thoroughly acquainted with them than any other form of visiting can do. In my case I found my first impressions but confirmed and widened. Not only apparently, but from more than one assurance of the fact, I know that the brothers worked together most harmoniously, and yet I think it would be difficult to find two men of more opposite characters. To be sure, both were true and just and energetic, with a high standard of morals and duty; but the elder brother, William, was far narrower in his sympathies, and far more rigid in his prejudices than Robert. I am afraid the elder was nearly pitiless to people who had brought their misfortunes on themselves by extravagance or even imprudence. Had he been a Pagan, I think he would have dedicated a temple to Thrift and worshipped in it. As in his autobiography he has related the early struggles of his family, it can be no breach of confidence for me to allude to them.

In the summer of 1845, William Chambers had a little house at Peebles, whither he and his wife occasionally went for a short interval, driving from their Edinburgh home in their own carriage. Thither they took me for a three days' sojourn in lovely July weather. It was in the drive to Peebles that we passed by the Lammermoor, and its weird and desolate appearance impressed me greatly. The imagination of genius is fired sometimes by trifling

incidents, and I can understand that the aspect of
that moor may have suggested to Scott the tragic
story, which to my mind remains his masterpiece.
It was a quaint little dwelling we occupied, where I
had the experience—and did not like it—of sleeping
in a recess in the old-fashioned Scotch manner.
Also the window of my room was of so primitive
a character that it had to be propped open with a
piece of wood. Nevertheless the time passed very
pleasantly, filling my mind with new ideas.

It must have been while we were at Peebles that
I was taken to see the hut of the unhappy deformed
creature whose character and appearance had suggested his "Black Dwarf" to Scott. Nearly all
readers of that powerful romance are, I suppose,
aware of the true story of the crippled and in many
ways misshapen man who thus kindled the sympathy
and imagination of the great author. Scarcely three
feet and a half high, with a ponderous head and an
active brain, maddened by the taunts and jeers of
the thoughtless and the cruel, he determined to
build for himself a moorland dwelling far away from
the haunts of man. I imagine this cave-like shelter
is still preserved as a show-place to tourists. As I
saw it in 1845 it more resembled the lair of a savage
beast than the home of a human being. This David
Ritchie too, though poor, was a man of some culture,
since he delighted in Milton's " Paradise Lost," and
also admired Shenstone's pastorals.

The hut, low-roofed and very small, was composed entirely of stones roughly put together. To the best of my recollection there was no flooring but the bare, hardened earth, which seemed undulating to the tread; but there was an attempt at producing what the Scotch call a "butt and a ben"! The little inner compartment, however, was hardly large enough to hold a comfortable bed, and I think it had not any door. The small garden had been walled round, for the poor solitary loved his garden, and made a little money out of it, but hated being looked at. Not that he refused help when it was offered to him—something I suspect he felt as if he were "spoiling the Egyptians." His companions were a dog and a cat, and he kept bees, which were profitable. When I saw the hut it was entirely empty, and the neglected garden—no doubt purposely neglected to render the show-place more picturesque and pathetic—instantly recalled to my mind a beautiful passage in Goldsmith's "Deserted Village"—

> " Where once the garden smiled,
> And still where many a garden flower grows wild."

Generally everything seemed choked and crushed for want of pruning and cutting away, but amid a briery tangle there had struggled forward, as if towards light and warmth, a blooming white rose which I obtained permission to appropriate. Dried and withered I know I kept it for years, but length

of days shows us how few things are quite im-
perishable !

Peebles was the birthplace of the brothers Chambers, and I was shown over the house in which they
were born. Also I was taken to the churchyard to
read the inscriptions on the tombs of their forefathers.
For many years they had been burghers of good
repute, honoured and esteemed in the town, but the
father of the brothers Chambers fell into difficulties
from trusting the French prisoners of war in the
neighbourhood to the amount, I think, of two or three
thousand pounds. Hence the migration of the family
to the neighbourhood of Edinburgh, when the elder
son was twelve years old. Certainly several generations of blameless ancestry must be an honour to any
one, and in that sense the Chambers were well born ;
but, while some other members of the family spoke
only vaguely of what they called the " dark ages,"
William Chambers liked, I think, to dilate on the early
struggles, though, I suppose, only to a sympathetic
listener, which I certainly was. He told me that
when a mere boy in a bookseller's employ he lived on
a very few shillings a week, saving money enough out
of that sum to buy a printing machine ; and, when
driving through Edinburgh, he often indicated spots
associated with those early years. I remember his
pointing out a doorstep, saying, " Look at that, I will
tell you something about it presently ; " and to a
certain house he pointed in a similar manner. Then

he told me he had sat crying on that doorstep because
he had lost a penny, not his own, and some kind old
gentleman, seeing his distress, had questioned him and
given him a penny. He had taken a parcel to the
house he indicated, with instructions to wait for an
answer, and while he waited the cook gave him an
ample dinner to beguile the time. In one of his
published reminiscences he alludes to the trivial sum
that had been paid for his education—something considerably under ten pounds—and how he had taught
himself to read French with the help of taking a
French Testament to kirk to follow the English
reading.

It must have been these early recollections which
made him, when a rich man, severe in his judgment
on all those who failed to live within their means,
whatever those means might be ; but that he had
deep feelings, though seldom displayed, beneath his
cold manners there is no doubt. There was one
anecdote, the memory of which touches me to this
day. When the humble shop-boy he had a Christmas
or New Year's present made him of half a guinea ;
it was a cold winter's evening, and his parents lived
four or five miles out of Edinburgh, but knowing
their pressing needs, and eager to bestow his treasure
on his beloved mother, he set off to do so. He found
the home fireless and dark ; the little family were all
in bed ; but he obtained admission, and made his way
through the darkness to his mother's bedside ; then

he told her of his good fortune, putting the coin into her hands. With emotion he described how she placed her hand on his head and solemnly blessed him. He trudged back to Edinburgh without breakfast, after a few hours of rest. I think he firmly believed that that blessing was heard, and had to do with his future prosperity.

And yet—such a contradiction is there in human nature—this man, who looked back on the gift of that half-guinea as one of the joys of his life, had the greatest objection to any one offering the poor unearned money. He took me to task for giving a cottager's little child a fourpenny-piece; not out of consideration for my purse, but because he maintained that such practices demoralized people. He was all for helping people to help themselves, and this he was often enough ready to do. Though I came to Edinburgh ostensibly for recreation and sight-seeing, he thought it highly desirable that I still should be earning money. A quiet room was set apart for my use, and I was quite expected to ply my pen from after the eight-o'clock breakfast till twelve o'clock or half-past. I liked the arrangement immensely, for I had plenty on my mind to do; but the fact was my host supplied me in a great measure with literary work, suggesting this and that I should write for the *Journal* or other publications. For instance, on one occasion he brought me the proof-sheets of one of the *Miscellany of Tracts* they were then publishing, but which proved to be five pages short of the thirty-two required. It was a story, and he suggested that I should look it through, and by inventing additional incidents, or by other means, bring it to the required length. I was a little dismayed, but, as the story was to appear anonymously, I thought the author—who turned out to be my friend, Dinah Mulock—would not be much injured. So I set to work, studied the thing one day, and the next added the five pages necessary by putting in additional paragraphs or sentences here and there. Thus I earned a couple of guineas, and in the course of the five or six weeks I stayed with Mr. and Mrs. William Chambers, I acquired, by various little articles or literary patch-work, much more than paid my expenses to and from Edinburgh. I relate this incident to show the manner in which William Chambers liked to serve one whom he considered rather as a *protégée.*

In that household everything passed off with the utmost regularity and precision, a state of things to which I could always pleasantly accommodate myself. At one o'clock the carriage was ordered, and Mrs. Chambers and I, after a slice of cake and a glass of wine, drove to the publishing place of business in the High Street to pick up her husband. Usually we got out for a while—perhaps he was not quite ready, perhaps there was something to show me—then we went sight-seeing till close upon four o'clock, the dinner hour. Of course I was taken to

G

see Holyrood, with all its memories of the unhappy
Mary Queen of Scots. I should, however, have been
but little instructed had I only depended on the
explanations of the established guide. This was
a voluble woman ; but she spoke such broad Scotch
that I did not understand a single word she said.
I have little doubt that William Chambers knew as
much about Holyrood as she could tell; but he
appealed to her frequently, speaking in exactly the
same manner as she did, then he would turn to me
interpreting ! I was astonished, wondering if this
broad Scotch could have been the "mother tongue"
of my host, for both he and his brother spoke
English with great accuracy, and only the little
"flavour" which proclaimed their nationality.

The dinner was always simple but excellent, and
it left us a long evening for conversation, or reading,
or needlework. Tea was brought to the drawing-
room, but we returned to the dining-room at ten
o'clock for a light supper, for several weeks chiefly
composed of strawberries and cream. I found the
Scotch custom was to shred the strawberries from
their tiny stalks and serve them in a tureen, to be
helped with a soup ladle in ample quantities. Instead
of dessert plates soup plates were used, and a large
jug of cream was always placed on the table. I
quite understood the approbation of the schoolboy
who exclaimed, "This is the place for strawberries ;
soup plates, and come twice."

This was the simple mode of living of the elder brother and his wife, at whose invitation it was that I went to Edinburgh, and passed several weeks under their roof. Already presumably a rich man, Mr. Chambers was destined to be the founder of the Chambers's Literary Institute, at Peebles, which he also endowed, and to be the restorer of St. Giles's Cathedral, in Edinburgh, besides retaining a noble fortune. The poor boy, who had worked his way up to honours and wealth, in later years became Lord Provost of Edinburgh, and died at the age of eighty-three, when just about to assume the dignity of a baronet, the patent being made out.

Knowing him and his wife as well as I did, I have sometimes wondered with what feelings they went through the duties and ceremonies of the Lord Provost's office. They seemed to me to absolutely dislike what is called "society;" and I do not remember more than one or two callers while I was with them, or a single guest at dinner. To me they were all kindness, showing me all they could think of that would interest me, not only in Edinburgh, but taking me to Abbotsford, Dalkeith, etc., and, on my way home, seeing me to Greenock by the route of the Trosachs, Loch Katrine, Loch Lomond, and Glasgow.

It must be worth while to contrast the Loch Katrine of those days with its troubled waters of the present time. We slept at Callander, and rose at five in the morning, so as to reach the shores of the lake by eight o'clock. There we embarked in a wherry rowed by two Highlanders, who to each other spoke Gaelic, but to us English, as if it were a foreign language acquired with some difficulty, and of which they possessed but a limited vocabulary. Their speech had but the merest trace of what we call Scotch accent. But facing the rowers for, I should think, a couple of hours, I observed their countenances, and noted how little labial the Gaelic was. They talked often to each other, but I think the upper and lower lips never met. When we reached "Ellen's Isle" and other points of interest they indicated them in good set English phrases. I hear that now Loch Katrine is ploughed by steamboats. On the summer morning of which I am writing the water was crystal-clear, refracting the oars, and we saw but two wherries besides our own, and a solitary angler on the shore.

But this was towards the end of my visit, and there was an interregnum of about ten days, during which I visited Mr. and Mrs. Robert Chambers. Just then their house in Edinburgh was undergoing repairs, and they occupied a commodious dwelling at Musselburgh, about five miles from the town. In depicting the different home-lives of the two brothers, I hope to indicate the different characters of themselves and their wives.

Without being at all a disorderly house, the

younger brother's establishment had a little touch
of the Liberty Hall about it.   In the first place, the
breakfast hour was nearer nine than eight; and,
though those who were the first of a large party
to assemble might have the hottest tea or coffee, the
late comer would, at any rate, not experience the
keen reproach of having been waited for.   It was
the same at luncheon—a substantial meal between
one and two o'clock.   The dinner hour must, I think,
have been six.   My host was usually, but not always,
away in Edinburgh the greater part of the day;
but there was always something going on—visitors
dropping in, or an excursion to be made, or some
subject of interest to be discussed.   Then there was
the houseful of happy, merry children, to whom
scolding seemed absolutely unknown, and a charming girl-governess, who was treated like a daughter
of the house.   As for Mrs. Robert Chambers, she
was the most genial of hostesses, with a sweet voice
that had music in it, thoughtful for others but contented in herself.   She told me that throughout her
happy married life—then a period of about sixteen
years—each year had been happier and more prosperous than its predecessor.   It is said that to every
earthly paradise the serpent winds its way—certainly
I never heard its hiss or saw its crest during my visit
to Musselburgh.   I remember Robert Chambers
alluding laughingly to his wife's "organ of benevolence," and saying that "if he were to set her up

in business she must inevitably be a bankrupt in six
months." People, especially the Scotch, more often
spoke "phrenologically" in those days than they do
at present.

In the evening we generally had music. The
eldest daughter was already a fine pianist, Mrs.
Robert played the harp, and the little girls sang
sweetly in chorus. Jacobite songs were greatly in
vogue, but not to the exclusion of "God save the
Queen," and some American ditties then newly
imported.

One day there was a dinner-party of ten or a
dozen, when a little incident occurred which seems
to me worth recording. When staying in Edinburgh
with the other couple my attention had been drawn
to a book recently published, which was making
some noise in the world, namely, "Vestiges of the
Natural History of Creation." William Chambers
had asked my opinion of it. What opinion I gave I
can but vaguely remember. I am only very sure
that I was not capable of forming one. At the
dinner-party, to which I allude, among the guests
were D. M. Moir—the "Delta" of *Blackwood's
Magazine*—and his wife, and Mrs. Crowe, the author
of "Susan Hopley" and "The Night Side of Nature."
I forget what other guests were present; but I
think it might be called a literary party. Just when
the fish was removed, the time when tongues are
loosened, "The Vestiges" came under discussion.

A quarter of lamb was set before the master of the house—for dinners *à la Russe* had not yet been introduced—and he was in the act of separating the shoulder from the ribs with the skilful dexterity of an accomplished carver, when some lady at the upper end of the table, with singular impropriety, exclaimed—

"Do you know, Mr. Chambers, some people say you wrote that book."

Though sitting next my host, I happened to be looking towards Mrs. Chambers, and I saw that she started in her chair and that a frown was on her face. She looked at her husband, but his eyes were bent on the lamb, on which he continued operating in an imperturbable manner, observing—

"I wonder how people can suppose that I ever had time to write such a book."

There was silence for a minute, and then I think the subject dropped.

I believe I have never since seen a quarter of lamb without thinking of that dinner and Robert Chambers's evasive answer. Now that the book is acknowledged to have been his, and his wife is stated to have been the copyist, I can well understand her start and her frown. Wonderfully well was the secret kept for nearly forty years, although rumour was rife in suggesting the author. For years the work was out of print, high prices being offered for a copy. But a mighty change came over the mind of Robert Chambers, from circumstances to which I shall have to allude by-and-by—a change which fully accounted for the suppression of the book.

The "Delta" of *Blackwood's* belonged to a generation of authors who have passed away, but he made his mark, and was a most cultivated man. He was a medical practitioner and a polished gentleman; I felt it a privilege to have known him.

In later years I often met Mrs. Crowe in society. She was an eccentric woman, not particularly refined, but at any rate she had the courage of her opinions.

I do not desire to obtrude personal details of my memorable visit to Edinburgh, yet I cannot describe the difference between the two brothers without alluding to myself. I do not think the younger brother thought it altogether good for me to have so much desultory literary work as circumstances forced upon me. He had much more sympathy with the struggles of authors than William had, having himself many more of their idiosyncrasies. Robert knew perfectly well that for important work great concentration of mind was necessary, and that petty tasks are ruinously distracting. He had imagination and sympathy, and one of the kindest hearts in the world. He appreciated everything that was fine in poetry and imaginative literature, and though not so rapid in his judgments as his brother, the comparative slowness was that of one who looks all round a subject before coming to a decision. His contributions to the *Journal* showed him to be a thoughtful essayist, and his biographical and historical writings proved how indefatigable a student he could be. He was a delightful companion, from whose conversation one always gained ideas.

William Chambers could also write well—but it must be on matters of fact. A story only pleased him if it illustrated some truth in which he believed. He had not the least understanding of poetry; confessed that he "could not see what there was in Shakespeare to make such a fuss about," and thought Longfellow's "Evangeline" "prose run mad." He seemed to have hardly any comprehension of the truths that are greater than fact, and was, I think, quite devoid of the sense of humour.

And yet, like every Scotchman I ever knew, he thought very much of Burns, and I was taken to Ayr to see the sister of the poet, Mrs. Begg, who was still surviving. Of course I saw also the house in which Burns was born, and the different objects associated with him, but the living relic was to me the most interesting. She was a handsome, somewhat stately old woman, of between sixty and seventy, strikingly like the engraving of her brother's portrait which hung over the mantelpiece of her little parlour. Her touch of stateliness was innate, and corresponded to the easy good manners which were quite devoid of affectation. I rather think Robert Chambers had exerted himself to obtain some small pension for her, and she lived with her daughter, a young woman of about eight-and-twenty, who was occupied as a dressmaker. She also resembled the poet, and had her mother's pleasant manners, with the addition of more cheerfulness.

I never could ascertain what quality it was in the poetry of Burns that William Chambers appreciated, and suspect he did not know himself. But the fact is that in Scotland Burns is "a name to conjure with." The brothers must often have differed in their opinions on literary matters. Once I myself wrote a story for the *Journal*, which was accepted by Robert with words of approbation; a few days later came a letter of regret that his brother did not agree with him as to its suitability for the *Journal*. On another occasion I pleased William with the manuscript I offered, while his brother thought less of it; but note, this story approved by William appeared after all, while the one Robert liked was returned to me. The fact was the younger brother in trifling matters yielded habitually to the elder; hence the concord of their lives.

Unquestionably William Chambers loved power, and I should say would never have got on well with relatives that thwarted him. Perhaps his nature would have been softened had his children lived, or had his wife drawn out and encouraged the latent tenderness in his nature. But she always seemed to me the reflex of her husband. I do not remember ever seeing her with a book in her hand, but she adopted all the opinions of her lord and master, so far as I could judge, because they were his, not for her own reasons. There are many men who admire this sort of wife more than any other; and, though they must be aware that it is but a parrot-voice they hear, are comforted by the sound.

I have alluded to the latent tenderness of William Chambers's nature; that he had it was proved by his love and reverence for his mother. I think it was Mrs. William Chambers who told me that during the illness which preceded her death, when her sons sought by every means to assuage her sufferings, she almost rebuked them for extravagance. The venerable mother who had suffered such straits in early life could not forget their lessons, or quite understand the changed condition of affairs. Especially she grieved over the cost of hothouse grapes that had been provided for her. "Mother," exclaimed her son, "if ten thousand pounds could do you good we could afford it."

Also William Chambers was full of pity and tenderness for animals, and, I believe, abhorred cruelty beyond any other vice. Three dogs reigned over his heart, like successive sovereigns, during about thirty years. I remember his coming to lunch with me soon after the demise of the second, and telling me the particulars of her sudden death. He used to pay the extra fare when he travelled that it might be with him in a first-class carriage. He was about

to leave Edinburgh for his country place, Glenormiston, when at or near the station the dog had
some seizure that was fatal.

"I wrapped it in my plaid," he said with a choking
voice, "and carried it on my knees, that it might be
buried at Glenormiston." Then he added, with the
tears in his eyes, and, I think, on his cheeks, "Oh, it
was terrible when I took off her beads!" The dog
wore a necklace instead of a collar. Happily this
was the last trial of that kind that he had, for the
next favourite to which he attached himself survived
his master.

This dog-love was no mere freak of declining years.
He wrote an imaginary autobiography of an earlier
pet, and had it printed as a specimen of most exquisite typography and exhibited in the Great Exhibition of 1851. He gave me a copy—which in subsequent years must have been stolen from me. The
loss was a lesson not to place a curiosity of literature
on an open bookshelf.

The brothers were Nature's gentlemen, and born
organizers and rulers. It was delightful to visit their
vast establishment and observe the respect in which
they were held and the exquisite order which prevailed. Though strict discipline was maintained, it
was tempered by great kindliness. I remember going
with William Chambers through a room where I
should think about sixteen or eighteen young girls
were working, their occupation entirely consisting in

folding printed sheets—so far as I observed mainly of the *Journal* and *Miscellany of Tracts*—pressing them down with a paper-knife. This they did with great rapidity, but several of the girls he stopped to praise with kindly words for the extra neatness of their work.

Towards the close of my visit, the annual entertainment to their workpeople took place, in which a few literary friends joined. I sat next to Professor Masson, then a very young man, not more than one-and-twenty I should think, but from his conversation I felt sure he was one who was to make his mark in the world. On that occasion, too, I think it was, that I was introduced to Mr. Wills, then recently engaged to Janet Chambers, one of whose bridesmaids I was the following year. She was the sister of William and Robert Chambers, but much their junior, and inherited a good share of the family talent, contributing from time to time sprightly articles to the *Journal*. At the period of her engagement her future husband was one of the literary employees of the firm. Before their marriage, however, he became the associate of Charles Dickens in various journalistic undertakings, working for many years very hard and successfully in his editorial capacity. Only in October, 1892, after a widowhood of many years, did Janet Wills pass away, beloved and lamented by a large circle of friends and relatives. A very genial and well-deserved notice of her appeared in the *Athenæum* for the 29th of the month in which she died.   She was indeed a woman of very rare qualities, both of heart and mind, yet so little assertive of herself that one needed to know her long and well to fully estimate her worth.   She was quickly appreciative of literary work, belonging to that high order of critics who look first for the merits of a book before noticing its faults.   She recognized the advantage she had had in mixing from her youth with intellectual people, whose society she enjoyed immensely, always upholding the influence of mentally endowed women.   She spoke from large and long experience.

As I write this of my dear old friend, I feel that the generation to which we belonged has almost passed away, and in recording circumstances associated with it I seem to be only rescuing a few spars from the wreck of long ago!

CHAPTER VII.

The annuals and the Countess of Blessington—Marguerite Power—
H. F. Chorley—Louis Napoleon—Gore House.

A YEAR or two before I commenced writing for
Chambers's Journal I began to contribute to two or
three of the leading annuals, feeling gratified, as I
am very sure many more experienced authors would
have been, by being allowed to do so. I want to
offer a defence of these publications, which it is now
the fashion to sneer at and scorn. They fell out of
favour, I am persuaded, not from deterioration of
quality, but because the era of cheap literature was
slowly advancing, and publishers could not pay
distinguished authors liberally, and engravers such
as the Findens and Heath, the high prices they
demanded, and compete with five-shilling Christmas
books, which were in a very few years to be superseded by shilling holiday numbers of magazines.

It was said that Sir Walter Scott received four
hundred guineas for the short story he contributed
to the first *Keepsake;* and, allowing for perhaps a
little exaggeration, there is no doubt he obtained a

large sum for the few pages from his pen which
appeared. It is within my own knowledge that for
many years authors were exceedingly well paid
when writing for or editing the annuals. It is easy
to talk of such and such an author giving but the
"sweepings of his study" to these richly illustrated
gift-books, but why should he have done so when
the guerdon was so satisfactory? Brief the articles
often were, but where goldsmiths work the dust is
of value. Publications with contributions by Bulwer-
Lytton, Walter Savage Landor, Mrs. S. C. Hall,
William and Mary Howitt, Disraeli, Lord John
Manners, the present Duke of Rutland, Mrs. Hemans,
L. E. L., Barry Cornwall, Mr. Ruskin—who did not
disdain *Friendship's Offering* as the vehicle for some
of his very early but really beautiful poems—and a
host of other writers of sterling merit could not be
worthless.

Another cause, little I suppose suspected by the
general public, conduced to the falling off in the
sale of the annuals, and this was the opening up
of what was called the overland route to India.
Calcutta, Bombay, and our Indian empire generally
afforded great markets for the annuals, and for this
reason a large number of copies had always been
got ready by the end of July, so as to be shipped
for the long voyage round the Cape, and yet arrive
at their destination in time for Christmas or New
Year's presents. But when communication between

India and England became more rapid and frequent, Anglo-Indians participated in the influx of cheap literature, and orders for expensive books fell off accordingly. Lieutenant Waghorn's indefatigable zeal appeared to have almost annihilated time and space in the days when a Suez Canal and submarine telegraphs would have been looked upon as fairy tales.

The annuals made me acquainted with several literary people, for I not only wrote in them for nearly twenty years, but for two years I was assistant or sub-editor of *Friendship's Offering.* The ostensible editor was Mr. Leitch Ritchie, an author distinguished in several departments of literature, but who at the time he was associated with *Friendship's Offering* was a good deal taken up with political writing. I suppose he thought me competent to the task when he proposed that I should receive a fair share of the editorial salary, and correspond with authors, correct proofs, read offered manuscripts, and arrange for the illustration of plates, or write for one, as I did when time pressed and there had been a disappointment.

My first experience, however, of writing to a plate had occurred two or three years previously, and had led to my personal acquaintance with Lady Blessington. From the year 1838, she had accepted little poems of mine for her *Book of Beauty*, always with gracious notes of acknowledgment ; but, in 1839 or 1840, she sent me the merest outline of a portrait, with a request that I would write a few verses to

H

it. I knew not what to do. The engraver's work
was not sufficiently advanced for me to divine
whether the face was full of dignity and intelligence,
or only revealed the beauty of youth ; of course one
of these attributes it must have been expected to
possess. I took counsel with one or two intimates
as to the propriety or prudence of my calling on
Lady Blessington instead of writing to her about the
plate, and the offer of a friend to drive me in her
carriage to Gore House decided the matter.

Many subsequent visits I paid, and one very
memorable one, but always was there the same
formality. The great carriage gates were always
shut, and it was some one from the stable who
answered the loud bell from a small side door. He
never knew if his mistress was at home, but took
the card that was presented, and in a few minutes
the visitor was admitted into the courtyard. The
hall door was flung wide open by a powdered footman in a gorgeous livery of green and gold, and the
name passed on to another servitor that looked in
every particular his counterpart ; both were certainly
upwards of six feet in height. This second footman
ushered me, on my first visit, into the library, where
the hostess advanced to meet me in the most cordial
manner possible. Explaining the object of my visit,
I gained all the information necessary, and, I believe,
had a more advanced sketch sent me ; at all events,
some lines of mine on a lady's portrait appeared in

the *Book of Beauty* for 1843. When I left, Lady
Blessington pressed my hand in both of hers, saying,
" Look upon me as an old friend," with words that
invited me to come and see her again. I own I
was gratified and charmed by my reception, and,
prudent or imprudent, I for some years made an
afternoon call at Gore House every few months.
Soon Lady Blessington became editress of the
Keepsake as well as of the *Book of Beauty*, and I
continued writing in both books.

It must have been not later than 1841 that I was
introduced to Marguerite Power, the niece who had
lately come to reside with Lady Blessington, and
henceforth I seemed to be considered the friend
of Miss Power, at least as much as of the elder lady.
I can understand the generous tact which made Lady
Blessington desire that this should be the case.

Marguerite Power was well known for many years
in a large literary circle in London first, and afterwards in Paris, and at the time I first knew her
must have been about nineteen years of age. She
was not strictly beautiful, though she had what
beauty sometimes lacks, a very sweet and winning
expression of face, and the good points of a graceful
figure, as well as a small white, well-shaped hand.
Altogether she attracted me greatly, and I grew to
like her very much. Though several years my junior,
I think she was older in knowledge of the world than
I then was. Her appearance was quite as youthful

as her stated age, but not so her manners. I never
saw in her the hopeful eagerness and buoyancy of
youth. I have seen her weep, but I never heard her
laugh. Whether this condition arose from some
early sorrow, from a touch of the lymphatic in her
temperament, or from some dim consciousness of
the cloud that hung over her surroundings, it would
be hard to say ; perhaps these causes all combined
to make her what she was—calm, earnest, and dignified, even in her girlhood. There is a portrait of
her in the *Book of Beauty* for 1842, which is a very
fair likeness. In the *Keepsake*, for 1849, she is again
seen, but representing here the heroine of one of the
stories. The usual tributary verses to the first-named
portrait were written by H. F. Chorley. They
begin—

> " A song for her ! whose life itself a lay
>   Of youth and joy and beauty ; . . ."

and one sighs, looking at the book half a century
old, to remember the sorrows and disappointments
that were in store for the blooming girl. Henry
Fothergill Chorley was a man who, for some thirty
years, held an established position in London literary
society, more, however, I think, as the musical critic
of the *Athenæum*, than for contributions to other
departments of literature. In later years I knew
him exceedingly well, having occasion to see him
at least once or twice a week for several months in
reference to literary work in which we were associated.

He was strictly honourable and reliable, but eccentric and "crotchety," and I think very proud of being able to criticise a new opera without taking notes during the performance. But, above all things, he was a "fine gentleman." I remember his telling me of having had occasion to call on L. E. L., and finding her at the street door taking in the milk. "I don't admire that sort of thing," he exclaimed, with a shrug of the shoulders, expressive of absolute disgust, which seemed intensified by the fact that Miss Landon did not look at all discomposed by the circumstance, merely observing that the one servant had gone out on an errand.

Gore House has long since been razed to the ground, but it still is occasionally mentioned—often by people who never entered its portals—as the meeting-place for some fifteen or eighteen years of the brightest spirits of the age. Yet I do not remember ever reading a description of the room in which Lady Blessington usually received her friends. Let me attempt one. I have already called it the library, and since the walls were almost entirely covered with books, it assuredly deserved the name. But the shelves, or at any rate the edges of them, instead of being dark, were of that enamelled white which looks like ivory, small interstices being filled up with looking-glass; the panels of the doors were also of looking-glass, and the handles glass.

It was a very large room on the right hand, enter-

ing the house, and, from its two fireplaces and supporting columns in the centre, had evidently been
originally two apartments.   It ran through the house
from north to south, the southern windows looking
out on the lovely garden, with its fine old trees.   It
was at this end of the room we always sat, though
the door from the hall was near the north windows.
The furniture was delicate, apple-green silk damask
set in white and gold, with fauteuils in abundance,
protected by the first antimacassars I ever saw—not
the abominations of crochet and knitting, but delicate
fabrics of muslin and lace.   The carpet was of a very
minute pattern, a shade darker than the furniture.
Summer and winter Lady Blessington always occupied
the same seat, a large easy-chair near the fireplace, with
a small table beside her, on which was probably a new
book with the paper-knife between the leaves, and a
scent-bottle and a fan.   Through all the years I knew
her she never varied her style of head-dress.   What
hair was visible was of a chestnut hue, braided down
the cheeks, while straight across the forehead, in what
I can only describe as the lady-abbess fashion, was a
piece of rich lace or blonde, but the same material
was brought down one side of the face and drawn
tight as if supporting the chin, and invisibly fastened
on the other side.   The lace set her face as if in a
frame, and hid many telltale lines of advancing
years.   No doubt Lady Blessington studied dress, as
every woman to a certain degree should do ; but she

never attempted to conceal her age, talking freely of the long ago and of Byron, whom of course she called *Birron.* She was about fifty when I first knew her, and very stout, a circumstance which she spoke of and lamented ; but she had the remains of great beauty, though her nose was slightly " tip-tilted." She had abundant command of language, speaking, in my opinion, more eloquently than she wrote, and in tones where now and then the delicate flavour of the Dublin accent could be detected—that accent which gives emphasis and expression to kind words, and is wholly different from what is called brogue. She told a good story capitally, and was quite the best *raconteuse* I ever heard.

She related to me a little anecdote of Mrs. Wyndham Lewis, who lived to be Viscountess Beaconsfield, and which I imagine she must have had from Disraeli, or perhaps from L. E. L. herself ; at any rate, she spoke of the circumstance as within her knowledge. The rich widow heard incidentally that Miss Landon was saving up her money to buy a black velvet dress, and the next day a present of twenty yards of Genoa velvet was sent to her in the most delicate manner, with expressions of regret that " L. E. L. should have wished for anything she could not obtain."

I do not doubt that the present was accepted as graciously as it was offered. Poor L. E. L.! who throughout her short life worked for others rather than herself; who once said that out of £400 she received for a book she bought for herself only a pair of gloves; who suffered from terrible headaches, but wrote verses, to keep her engagements with publishers, with wet bandages across her forehead! Perhaps she is as much depreciated now as she was overlauded in her lifetime. But hers was a developing genius; her latest work was her best, and she died at six and thirty, before her mind had really ripened. Her fate seems to me quite as sad as that of Keats.

Lady Blessington was a staunch Buonapartist, and often spoke of Queen Hortense, whom she seemed to have known well. One day she mentioned that she had a very beautiful ring which the great Emperor had given to his step-daughter, adding, "Would you like to see it?" Of course I said "Yes," and she rang the bell which was at her elbow, and asked for her maid, to whom she gave a key and instructions.

I do not presume to be a great judge of gems, but much as I had always admired the sapphire, I never imagined it could be so beautiful as the one surrounded by diamonds which was shown to me. The blue translucent depth of the water was a thing to remember for ever; but though set as a ring, it was far too large to be appropriately worn as such by ordinary mortals, having the dimensions of a fair-sized brooch. I have often thought I should like to have known the history of that jewel, but Lady Blessington only mentioned it as having been the gift of the first Napoleon to

Queen Hortense, who, I suppose, presented it to its then owner. It might have been the ecclesiastical ring of some high functionary in the Romish Church, or have adorned the image of some patron saint; in either case it was, perhaps, the spoil of the unscrupulous conqueror. It must have been worth hundreds of pounds. I wonder at the Gore House wreck what became of it!

I remember some few months before Bulwer Lytton published his "Children of Night," Lady Blessington told me the sort of subject on which he was engaged. It was *à propos* of showing me the portrait of a niece then at the antipodes, a younger sister of Miss Power, and which was painted by the notorious convict, Thomas Griffiths Wainewright, sentenced to transportation for life for forgery, which he confessed, and suspected of poisoning his uncle, and his wife's sister for the sake of the insurance he had effected on her life. At one time this man was well known in literary and artistic circles, writing in the *London Magazine* under the name of "Janus Weathercock." By those who had known him he was reported to have been a man of mediocre, but varied and serviceable talents, devoured by conceit, and a fop in dress and manners. When he was taken on board the convict ship he endeavoured, but without effect, I suppose, to soften the hearts of the authorities, exclaiming, " I, who have been accustomed to the society of poets and philosophers, to herd with such as these ! "

The portrait that was shown to me was something in the style of Alfred Chalon, but wanting that last refining touch of ineffable grace which, notwithstanding their mannerisms, rendered the portraits by the French artist so charming.

Long before his conviction and transportation Wainewright's character was so suspected that he had gone abroad, and had been half forgotten by his former friends; but Dickens somewhere relates that when he was going over Newgate, with Macready and Barry Cornwall, the two latter were suddenly shocked by recognizing Wainewright among the prisoners as a man whom they had not only met in society, but at whose table, in the year 1821, they had sat, meeting there Hazlitt and other celebrities. Fifty or sixty years ago convicts of exceptional ability in New South Wales were often treated leniently, hence the circumstance that Wainewright had been allowed to occupy himself as an artist. I heard so much of his history at Gore House that I was a little disposed to write a magazine article about him ; but before I had put pen to paper Miss Power sent me a letter of the convict's wife to read, which touched me so much that I refrained from my purpose. I forget to whom the letter was addressed, but to one of the Power family, I think, who had taken an interest in and done some kindness to the miserable, heart-broken woman. I never read anything which, in fact or in fiction, so revealed the consciousness of hopeless degradation ; and it would have been cruel *then* to keep alive the story of her misery ; but nearly half a century has elapsed, and in the course of nature she must have passed from the scene of her anguish to the sphere where the sorrow-stricken are comforted and tears are wiped away.

Some years later I knew the original of the convict's portrait when her mother brought her to England. She was a charming and accomplished girl ; but, like her sisters, spoke with a peculiar drawl, evidently acquired from her mother, in whom it was still more pronounced. I remember it in another family with which in childhood I was acquainted, and have sometimes wondered whether it was a survival of what in the last century was called the Devonshire drawl, not, I fancy, from any resemblance to the west-country dialect, but from the affectation of an exclusive coterie.

I am tempted to describe one of my visits to Gore House rather circumstantially, chiefly because I saw there a world-famous man. I am nearly sure it was on the 1st of August, 1846. At all events it was a day about that period, a day memorable for one of the most violent storms of thunder and lightning and rain ever known in London. The weather in the morning was real summer weather, suggestive to the feminine mind of muslin dresses, so delightful to wear when the temperature permits, lessening fatigue to the non-

robust very perceptibly. I had made up my mind
to call on Lady Blessington, and though, as the day
went on, the heat increased, there seemed nothing
in the weather to thwart my intention. I arrived
at Gore House about three o'clock, I forget how,
probably by omnibus, getting out a hundred yards
from my destination. I might have been chatting
with Miss Power for about a quarter of an hour
when a low sound of thunder attracted us, and in
a few minutes it became evident that a storm was
at hand. It proved of the most violent character,
doing damage, an account of which filled the newspapers the next day. After a little while the rain
came down in torrents, drenching the garden that
we looked out upon, and forming rivulets in every
direction. It was weather in which, according to
the proverb, you would not turn your enemy's dog
out of doors. (N.B.—We might perhaps like our
enemy's dog better than its master.) It was before
the storm had much abated that Miss Power was
called out of the room ; but in a very few minutes
she returned, saying, " My aunt begs that you will
stay to dinner. We shall be quite alone, only Count
D'Orsay and ourselves."

What could I do but accept the impromptu invitation gratefully ! Dinner was not until eight o'clock,
and unthought of as yet was the five-o'clock tea,
so there was a long interval to pass somehow. I
had a better opportunity of noticing works of art,

or articles of interest scattered about the tables, than I had ever had before, and I grew, I think, more and more able to appreciate the fine taste which pervaded the apartment. There was no one mass of looking-glass or very striking object to distract the attention on entering the room from its human occupants, though when sought for there was abundance to charm. I suppose different people feel local influences differently, one person being contented in a dwelling in which another could not but be miserable. None can tell what may have happened in that library; but my feeling about it was of a place sacred to kindly thoughts and kindly speech, where bright ideas had birth, and angry words were never spoken.

I should mention that the drawing-room led out of the library by a masked door, and was reached by three steps down. I was shown it one day for the sake of the pictures, and found it a spacious, magnificent room looking out on the garden. It was loftier than the rooms level with the hall, perhaps by means of the lower flooring.

Of course I was in mere morning costume—a muslin dress, which fortunately was fresh, though of the simplest character. Half an hour or more before dinner-time Miss Power took me to her room to wash my hands and smooth my hair, and make my toilet as presentable as circumstances permitted; and now it was that I was struck by an instance of

good breeding, which must be my apology for these
personal details.   On the bed was laid out a pretty
dinner dress, and Henriette, the French maid, was
in attendance ; but Miss Power turned to her and,
speaking in French, intimated that she was not
going to change her dress.   So Miss Power retained
her morning dress of simple white that she might
keep her guest in countenance.   It was surely one
of those acts of true politeness the springs of which
are real kindliness and thoughtfulness.

   At this time the younger sister, Ellen Power, was
an invalid, so that she did not join us at dinner.
We formed a party *carré*—Lady Blessington, Count
D'Orsay, Marguerite Power, and myself.   I had heard
much of Count D'Orsay, but had never seen him ;
and, as he gave me his arm from the library to the
dining-room, I could not but feel how strange was
the accident which had placed me in my present
position.   There is no denying that I was interested
in seeing for myself a phase of the domestic life
which had been so much talked about, since the
opportunity seemed as it were to have been forced
upon me.   The dinner was, of course, a refined one,
though without being very elaborate ; and it was so
soon over that we had returned to the library and
were having coffee before half-past nine o'clock.
Shortly after this time "Le Prince Louis Napoleon"
was announced, and there entered the man lately
escaped from Ham, who was considered by the

generality of people as only a poor vain creature,
hardly worth the trouble of making a prisoner ; but
who was destined in a few years to be our "faithful
ally," to reach imperial dignity, and to be for nearly
two decades the most commanding figure on the
continent of Europe. Yet was he doomed to fall
tragically, and die in exile.

The Prince was received by his hostess and Count
D'Orsay with the quiet cordiality which marked him
as the intimate friend and *habitué.* Lady Blessington
occupied her usual chair. I sat near her, and the
visitor took the easy-chair on the opposite side of
the wide fireplace, D'Orsay drawing his own chair
near him, while Miss Power remained between me
and the Count. The Prince, speaking in French,
addressed himself chiefly to D'Orsay, and in a
lugubrious tone, for he seemed to be speaking much
of his father, for whom he was in deep mourning,
marked by his crape-covered hat ; but I heard little,
for Lady Blessington and Miss Power continued
talking to me. Still I turned my eyes sometimes
on the new-comer, whom I certainly thought one of
the ugliest men I had ever seen. His nose seemed
enormous, and his eyes sunken and small. His
complexion was so darkly sallow that it reminded
me of Carlyle's description of "the sea-green
Robespierre." Nevertheless I admired his simple
manners, which were more like those of an English
gentleman than what we used to associate with a

Frenchman. There was no more gesticulation or emphasis of speech than is becoming.

Earlier in the evening it had been arranged that a cab should be sent for to take me home, and at ten o'clock it was announced. After making my adieux, I was followed into the hall by Miss Power, who intimated to me that the cab was one which Count D'Orsay had used all day, and that consequently there would be nothing to pay. It was impossible for me to do anything but express my acknowledgments, but I laughed to myself at the kind-hearted subterfuge, and the very pale-coloured fib which had been told to spare my pocket. The idea of the elegant, over-fastidious Count D'Orsay having employed a four-wheeler for the day seemed to me ludicrous. I enjoyed my drive from Kensington to the Hampstead Road in the fresh night air that followed the storm, none the less because I had not to pay for it.

Within a fortnight from this time I received an invitation to again dine at Gore House. It was a short notice, one day for the next, and the pretext was to meet Mr. Bentley, whom Lady Blessington thought it would be advantageous to me to know personally. I was ill at the time, suffering from neuralgia, and I knew that many of my friends would shake their heads at my accepting this invitation. But I felt keenly that I *must* go. It seemed to me that, remembering the former hospitality, it would have been the height of rudeness and ingratitude to refuse. And then how dare I say that it was not fit for me to visit the home of two young girls like Marguerite Power and her sister, whose residence with their aunt, it seemed to me, ought to have quieted slanderous tongues?

The true story of poor Lady Blessington's life is little likely ever to be known. What I have heard I have gleaned from various sources, notably from one who knew a great deal about her, nearly twenty years before the time of which I am telling. That she was almost literally sold by her drunken father, an Irish squire, when she was little more than a child, and married to Captain Farmer at the age of fifteen, is, I believe, a fact. That the husband was even more vicious and brutal than the father, was likewise well known—so that the young wife separated from him before she was twenty. Some seven years later, after the death of her worthless husband, she married Lord Blessington. And it may be that trials and temptations, which would make the very angels weep, beset her in the intervening years; but no one doubts that she was a faithful wife to Lord Blessington. After his death, her intimate association with Count D'Orsay was imprudent, but I can easily believe that it grew out of a complication of circumstances.

Foreigners seem to think more than we do of family ties, such as that which existed in the present case, for D'Orsay was the husband of Lord Blessington's daughter by his first wife; but the marriage was an unhappy one, ending in separation. Lady Blessington must have been twelve or fourteen years older than D'Orsay, and their manner was very much that of mother and son.

Count D'Orsay's house was a small bachelor's residence next to Gore House; but I heard that there was a garden communication between the two, and that his studio was in the basement of Gore House. I can only say that in all my intercourse with Lady Blessington I cannot recall a word from her lips which conveyed an idea of laxity of morals, while very often her advice was excellent. She was always in a high degree generously sympathetic with the struggling and unfortunate, not in words only, but in actions, for she would take a great deal of trouble to do a small service, and was a kind friend to many who were shy of acknowledging their obligation.

But this is a long digression from the little dinner-party to which I had been invited. The next arrival to myself, following me by only a few minutes, was Lord Strangford, the sometime diplomatist, and translator of Camoens, at this time an elderly man, and the father of the Percy Smythe who was associated with the Young England party. I noticed that as he took Lady Blessington's hand he bowed over it, touching it with his lips with that old-fashioned courtesy which soon became rare. There was not a trace of affectation in his easy yet dignified manners—manners which seemed natural to the scholarly man of the world accustomed to the atmosphere of courts, and which contrasted very favourably with the bearing of Count D'Orsay. At dinner I sat between the two.

D'Orsay was considered a handsome man, and the leader of fashion in men's attire. He was tall, and with a good figure and carriage, and had fine hazel eyes, but he had one great defect, which made me wonder he was so much admired. His teeth had gaps between them, which caused his smile to degenerate into something approaching a sneer; and his hands, large and white and apparently soft, had not the physiognomy which pleases the critical observer and student of hands. I thought his conversation commonplace; but perhaps, though he spoke English fluently enough, his vocabulary of the language was somewhat limited. He struck me as being mannish, rather than manly, and yet with a touch of effeminacy quite different from that woman-like tenderness which adds to the excellence of a man. I think the characteristics to which I have alluded often distinguish the self-indulgent, and, whatever his talents and accomplishments, there can be no doubt that Count D'Orsay was without principle, or even the worldly prudence, which sometimes is the poor substitute for conscience.

I wonder if it is worth recording that a large French poodle belonging to Count D'Orsay was said to have suggested the principal dog in Landseer's "Laying Down the Law." I believe it was this poor animal which met with a sad end, dying in consequence of injuries received from Lady Blessington treading on it in the dusk as it lay at the foot of the stairs. One can imagine how like a white mat it might have appeared.

Mr. Bentley, the publisher, and Miss Power and her sister Ellen—there is a portrait of the latter, after Landseer, perhaps a trifle idealized, in the *Book of Beauty* for 1843—made up the little dinner-party. When we returned to the library, Mr. Bentley entered into conversation with me ; but it was chiefly about Lady Blessington and her books, dilating on the eagerness with which her works were read. As this statement implied commercial success with regard to them, it was a very satisfactory one to hear from her publisher.

Not very long after this dinner-party I thought it right to pay my respects by calling at Gore House. As latterly had been usual, I was received by Miss Power, who after a little while was called out of the room, as she had been on a former occasion ; when she returned, it was as before, with a message from her aunt, asking me to stay to dinner, saying they expected Prince Louis Napoleon, Lord Brougham, Mr. Disraeli, and some other friends, whom perhaps

I should like to meet. Under ordinary circumstances I am not quite sure what I should have done ; but I had never thought of such a proposition as this in pleasant weather, and it so happened that I considered myself pledged to be at home that evening, as Mr. and Mrs. William Chambers, who were in town, had promised to drop in at teatime if they could one evening that week—if they did not hear from me of any engagement. I explained the case to Miss Power, with due acknowledgments and expressions of regret ; but I had no alternative. I could not pass a slight on my kind Scotch friends. I was never again invited to dinner, though I called occasionally at Gore House as before. Almost, if not quite always, it was only Miss Power I saw ; but when Christmas came round I received, as I had done for many years, a present from Lady Blessington, usually of jewellery. It was in this way she requited many of her contributors, for the evil days had set in when the publishers were more parsimonious than of old.

I have often thought that it was all for the best that I could not stay to dinner on the occasion to which I have referred. I might have been drawn into the vortex of the Gore House set a great deal more than was good for me ; but it pained me to fancy that I might have been suspected of only fabricating an excuse.

In 1848 I married, and henceforth, living farther

from London than formerly, I only saw Miss Power
once for several years. If I remember rightly, it was
in the early spring of 1849 that the crash came, and
the contents of Gore House were sold by auction ;
and for the few months remaining of her life, Lady
Blessington resided in Paris. She must have felt
bitterly leaving her charming home—a necessity,
it was supposed, entailed by her having made herself
responsible for some of Count D'Orsay's debts.
However, Miss Power, in writing to me, made the
best of everything, saying how fond her aunt was of
Paris, and how much less fatiguing than formerly
her life would now be. But she lived only till the
summer of 1849, dying suddenly in the June of that
year. Miss Power told me that they had been
dining the evening before with Count D'Orsay's
nephew, the Duc de Guiche, and as it was a warm
summer moonlight night, and their residence was
not far distant, they walked home. The walk, however, and the climbing some stairs which followed,
proved too much for Lady Blessington's weak heart.
She had a sudden seizure which carried her off the
next morning, at the age of sixty.

No doubt the accession to power of Louis Napoleon,
to whom for years she had been a kind friend, had
something to do with her settling in Paris ; and it is
said that he was anything but pleased at the step she
had taken. The story goes that he asked her how
long she intended to remain in Paris, and that she

replied by the question, "Et vous, monseigneur?"
She was quite equal to making the retort; but I
think myself she had too much worldly wisdom to
do so. Besides, she was a staunch Buonapartist, and
had faith in the family star. Possibly, however, she
had experienced some disappointment during her
sojourn in Paris, which, coming on the break-up at
Gore House, had helped to undermine her health.

Marguerite Power carried on the editorship of the
Keepsake for several years, and wrote a touching and
graceful preface to the forthcoming volume, just
ready for the press when Lady Blessington died.
I saw her when she came to London for a brief stay
some time afterwards, and I believe all her friends
understood how important it was that she should be
able to carry on the annual. I think nearly if not
quite all the eminent people who had written for it
under Lady Blessington's editorship, continued their
aid under that of her niece, and the seven volumes
which ensued afford to this day very pleasant reading,
contrasting, in my opinion, most favourably with
most of the modern holiday numbers of periodicals.
Articles for the best annuals—whether they were
paid for by a publisher's cheque or not—were always
written for educated and cultivated readers. If a
classical or mythological allusion or reference to
the world-famous *belles lettres* was made, there was
reliance it would be understood; whereas when the
flood of literature for the masses set in, a different

order of things began to prevail. I remember the editor of a highly successful cheap publication saying to me, in reference to what I was doing for him, " Do not appear to teach, but at the same time do not give your readers credit for knowing anything."

When the cheap literature clamoured for the mastery, it began to be the fashion to call the annuals " elegant " productions, and thoughtful but refined writers " elegant authors," distorting a fine word from its old and right meaning. Lowell, in his "Fable for Critics," castigates Poe for applying some such epithet to Longfellow, saying—

" Remember that elegance also is force ; "

and many and many an " elegant " *Keepsake* article is far stronger in the sense of truth and purity than the coarse sensationalism which has crept into favour.

After her aunt's death, Marguerite Power lived chiefly in Paris ; and I had the gratification of being able to help her a little in the production of the *Keepsake*, as there were some difficulties in proof-correcting and corresponding with authors in the days when postal communication was not so rapid as at present. Looking over these old books, my impression is confirmed that she had more true literary ability than her aunt ; her poems are something more than graceful, and her prose is always thoughtful, with the flowing rhythm of balanced

periods that makes her style the opposite of
amateurish. I maintain that it was not in the falling
off of its contents that the *Keepsake* ceased with the
volume for 1857. That volume contained a charming
lyric by Elizabeth Barrett Browning, some lines by
her husband, a delightfully characteristic article on
Uttoxeter by the author of the "Scarlet Letter," an
alpine sketch by Albert Smith, and contributions
by Barry Cornwall, Owen Meredith (the second Lord
Lytton), and other writers fully worthy of being
placed beside them. Of course the engravings were
worthy of Heath. Also, during her editorship, Miss
Power enlisted the services of Thackeray, H. F.
Chorley, Tennyson, Mrs. S. C. Hall, Eugene Sue,
Madame Emile de Girardin, and de Lamartine; the
little French articles being a pleasant innovation.

I think it a debt due to Marguerite Power to dwell
on her merits, for her life had surely pathetic aspects.
I am afraid the cessation of the *Keepsake* was, in a
pecuniary sense, a great trouble—for I know that
soon afterwards her circumstances were painfully
narrow; also, I fear, her sister Ellen becoming a
Roman Catholic and taking the veil, must have been
a great sorrow to her. Ellen Power's conversion to
Romanism was said to be owing to her intimacy with
Mademoiselle de Praslin, who was so terribly orphaned,
and who took refuge from her anguish in the austeri-
ties of her religion. But I think it was Marguerite
herself who wrote me word that her sister's health

had broken down under the discipline of the convent, and that she had obtained a dispensation for a few weeks to take her to Boulogne with the hope of benefiting her. I have to confess that after a time our correspondence languished—not, I am sure, from decay of friendship, but because we were far apart in separate circles, and were both too busy to write needless letters. Happily, Marguerite Power made and kept many friends, and with some of these she travelled to the East. But she was already in failing health, partly, I heard, in consequence of a fall from a pony, from which she never recovered. Possibly it was in one of her last letters she told me she had been within sight of the Pyramids, without being well enough to reach them. Perhaps she mentions this circumstance in her graphic book, "Arabian Days and Nights," which was the result of her expedition. Her death was lamented by many friends.

CHAPTER VIII.

The "forties" continued—Mr. and Mrs. S. C. Hall—Thomas Moore—
  Jenny Lind—Rosa Bonheur—The author of "John Halifax,
  Gentleman," etc.

IT was in the spring of 1842 that I had the good
fortune to be introduced to Mrs. S. C. Hall; and,
happily for me, mere acquaintanceship soon passed
into a friendship that brightened my life. She was
then in the zenith of her popularity, for her best
novels and her admirable Irish stories were already
before the world; but, though the outside public
might from her books gain some idea of the writer,
it required intimate personal knowledge to form anything like an estimate of her many great qualities.
For my own part I cannot imagine a character more
finely balanced, and in this balance lay her strength
and her influence. She called herself an Irishwoman,
but her mother, Mrs. Fielding, whom I well remember
as a very cultivated old lady, was of Swiss Huguenot
extraction, and I was told that on her father's side
Mrs. Hall claimed some collateral relationship to
Henry Fielding the novelist. The first fifteen years
of her life were spent in Ireland, but, except in her

love of that country, her appreciation of the best points of the Irish character, her ardent endeavours to amend its faults, and benefit the people in days when they had a few things of which to complain, she was as little what we are accustomed to call Irish as any one I ever knew. She was not voluble of speech, though what she said was sure to be to the purpose ; she was also eminently just as well as generous, her generosity extending to taking much trouble for those she desired to serve. Conscious, as she once owned she was, of her "own value in the Row," she was the least egotistic of authors, and the most keenly appreciative of every sort of merit. Yet she never indulged in "blarney," but on the contrary, where from difference of age or circumstances advice was becoming, she would point out a fault or shortcoming with love and candour. Clearseeing in judging of character, though always inclined to think the best, she was unwavering in her attachments when once formed. If I seem to exaggerate, let me repeat what one, who had known her even longer than myself, said, as summing up her character after her death in 1881—"Mrs. Hall was an angel."

Her husband, Samuel Carter Hall, the art critic and prolific writer, who gave his reminiscences to the world, was entirely of English extraction, but he always struck me as being intensely Irish in character. Much of his early life was passed in the Emerald Isle, his father, an officer in the army, having

been quartered there. S. C. Hall did not always
let "discretion wait" upon "the valour" of his warm
impulsive heart, and got himself misunderstood and
into scrapes accordingly. Those, however, who knew
him best had the greatest respect and warmest regard
for him. Both were born in 1800, so that they were
forty-two when I first knew them, and I thought
him one of the handsomest men I had ever seen—
only the iron-grey of his hair indicating that he was
not a much younger man. When many years more
than fourscore I can only describe him as beautiful.
Mrs. Barnard, so well known in art circles, painted
him at this period, with his long white locks falling
over his shoulders, and the portrait is lifelike.

Mrs. S. C. Hall must have been very pretty when
young, and at all ages had a fine expression of
countenance, though perhaps her forehead was a little
too massive to harmonize with the general idea of
feminine beauty. There are many excellent photo-
graphs of her, but the painting by McIan, taken
when she was about eight and thirty years of age,
represents her most truly as what she appeared for
the next few years. In those days photography was
not, but many of the engravings from McIan's
portrait must be in existence, though probably not
in the possession of the original owners.

When I first knew the Halls they occupied a
charming little house at Brompton, called the
Rosery, from the flowers which in the blooming

season almost covered the front of it. A cottage *orné* it certainly was, with, for its size, a rather spacious hall, where always there were works of art to arrest the eye. To the right was the dining-room, which opened into a much larger apartment, the drawing-room. A baize door masking an inner door led from the drawing-room to Mrs. Hall's study, which I believe had been built for her at the side of the original dwelling with a thick wall facing the road. For Mrs. Hall was one of the brain-workers who could only work in absolute silence and freedom from distraction, and it was her habit to avoid morning conversation, and breakfast in her dressing-room, then give instructions for the day to her servants, and pass into her study at ten o'clock, where on no pretence was she to be interrupted. If letters came they were to be reserved for her until two o'clock, when her morning's work would be done. The study, as well as the drawing-room, looked out on a large, well-kept old-fashioned garden, such as many of the dwellers in far more pretentious abodes might envy. The aspect being north, with no glittering sunshine to disturb and distract, I can well understand the calm so necessary for concentrated thought that Mrs. Hall found in her study. She herself told me how necessary absolute quiet was to her, contrasting her own idiosyncrasy with that of Miss Edgeworth, who always wrote in the family sitting-room, amid the chatter and going and coming of the family. Mrs. Hall venerated Miss Edgeworth, whom she knew well, and she had once an interview with Hannah More, whom she described as a little old woman dressed in green, and courteous and kindly.

For many years Mrs. S. C. Hall was always "at home" on Thursdays in the afternoon till about five o'clock, and from seven or eight o'clock until eleven. Hours were much earlier in those days, and the Halls especially made a stand against late entertainments. They tried to set an example, but failed, I fear, in being followed, by always arriving at parties as nearly as possible at the hour the invitation named, and resolutely leaving about eleven. It was well understood that they did not wish their own guests to prolong their stay into the small hours, and so unfit them for the next day's duties.

In the "early forties" London life, in what may be called the upper or gentle middle-class, moved in altogether a different groove from what it does now. People of letters, and artists especially, very often dined at four and five o'clock, or even earlier, and frequently there were early social gatherings of congenial friends, where the entertainment was informal and inexpensive ; but, of all such, I remember none so delightful as those at the Rosery. Let me describe a few of the personages I met on these occasions.

One evening in 1843, Mrs. Hall brought up to me

to introduce a tall slender girl of seventeen, with graceful mien and fine grey eyes that, once seen, were not to be forgotten. They always seemed to be looking out on objects more serene than those before her. This was Dinah Maria Mulock, then a young aspirant, full of hero-worship of the great and good of every order, and destined to be known as the author of " John Halifax, Gentleman," and one of the most successful novelists of her day. I lost sight of her for a time, but some two or three years later we became very intimate. She consulted me about adopting literature as an earnest pursuit, and I had seen such indications of her genius that I gave her the warmest encouragement. There was something very interesting about her, and she had the faculty of quickly making friends. I remember taking her with me as an uninvited guest to a *conversazione* at the Westland Marstons, I being sufficiently intimate with them to venture on such a liberty, and feeling well assured they would like to know her. The result even exceeded my expectations; by the end of the evening she seemed to have won their hearts, and before a month had passed she was looked on as an *habituée*, welcome at all seasons. It was a friendship that had happy results, winning her many influential literary friends.

Sometimes there were evenings at the Rosery, for which express invitations were sent, and at one of these, in 1845, I met Thomas Moore, and thought it a high honour to be introduced to him. At this time he was sixty-five years of age, carrying his years well. Yet there was a weather-beaten look about his face that generally adds to the appearance of age. I was very familiar, through engravings, with the face of the Irish poet, and certainly the painters who had taken his likeness had been eminently successful, catching the expression of his countenance and that peculiar turn of the head which gave the look which, in a soldier, would be called "attention." Of course he was the observed of all observers, and I had plenty of time to notice him. After awhile Mrs. Hall took my hand rather suddenly, raising me from my chair, and, drawing me a few paces to where Mr. Moore was standing, said playfully, "Here is another." He put out his hand and smiled, and spoke a few pleasant words, I believe, as I suppose he had already done to twenty people— and I confess that to this day I like to remember that I have shaken hands with the author of the surely deathless "Irish Melodies," of the admirable "Life of Byron," of the too little-known poem, "My Birthday," and of "Lalla Rookh," which, in my youth, I was romantic enough greatly to enjoy. Unquestionably it has merits of Eastern colouring, purity of sentiment, and brightness of fancy and imagination, of which a mature critic may approve ; not to mention the delightful humour with which the character of Fadladeen is sustained. But Moore was something

K

besides a poet, and I feel that even under the roof of his old friends he would rather have had a quiet talk with any sensible person, on any sensible subject, than have been made the "lion" of a party.

I may mention here a circumstance which Mr. Hall related twenty years later. Walking in the garden with Tom Moore, when he was quite an old man, the subject of Little's "Poems" came up, and the poet shed tears while reflecting on the "sin of his youth." I wonder if certain writers of the present day will ever have the grace to do the like!

I have alluded to Mr. S. C. Hall having been frequently misunderstood. By indomitable energy and perseverance he had carried to a successful issue so many difficult undertakings that his sanguine nature made him sometimes over confident as to his power of bringing to maturity embryo schemes. Ideas were started which other people took up, and when he claimed to have been the original suggester, he was not always believed. But if his mind was not as evenly balanced as that of his wife, he had many of her fine qualities. As, at the time of his death, a writer in the *Standard* said, "Their business and employment in life was to do good and promote good by taking interest in all that can make men and women wiser, happier, and better." They did this not only by their pens, but by the exercise of that personal influence which circumstances placed largely in their power.

To Mr. S. C. Hall a debt of gratitude is due from the public at large for at least forty years of strenuous exertion in elevating among all classes their standard of Art. I am old enough to remember the false taste which prevailed, and the really hideous objects which in daily use were tolerated among a class —since so instructed—that is now quick to recognize the fitting and the beautiful. Mr. Hall, through the medium of the *Art Journal,* was a great factor in working the change. Not only was he quick in recognizing artistic talent, and giving it the help of praise and publicity, but from a very early period he made it his aim to cultivate the taste of the poor and lowly for "things of beauty," that should confer on them a pure pleasure untasted before. Of course we know the beauty and value of old china; but sixty years ago the beautiful in pottery was always the costly. It is not so now, at any rate so far as form is concerned; and Mr. Hall did much to stimulate manufacturers of all descriptions to employ true artists for designers, and produce cheap articles which should still be graceful.

No wonder the Halls had a large circle of friends and acquaintances, and that weekly receptions, during a great part of the year, were in a measure necessary to hold it together. Of course the people who had general invitations did not avail themselves of their privilege too often, or a crowd would certainly have overflowed into the highway or garden; but those meetings were delightful, nevertheless. Numerous artists, Royal Academicians, and others were among the usual guests, and I have often listened with great interest to discussions that were going on concerning new pictures or statues. Authors already famous—or destined to be so—were sure to be present, with, perhaps, two or three personages with "handles to their names," who liked such society, and it might be two or three eminent publishers.

One little anecdote I will mention, because it so well illustrates Mrs. Hall's kindliness of nature and excellent common sense. Some lady—I really forget who it was—to whom I had been introduced one evening by Mrs. Hall, asked me to visit her. Of course I duly acknowledged her courtesy ; but in the course of the evening I mentioned the circumstance to our hostess, saying, I suppose, "Would you like me to go ?" or something equivalent, to which Mrs. Hall replied, with a half-scolding smile—

"My dear, I am never guilty of the absurdity of bringing people together and then trying to keep them apart."

How pleasant these words made all future gatherings under that hospitable roof ; for I was destined to make many warm friends whom I had first met at the Rosery !

When I went alone to the Thursday evenings, as I sometimes did, Mrs. Hall always provided me with an escort as far as Sloane Street, there to see me into a vehicle which should take me home; for these meetings were not full-dress affairs, and many of the lady guests came in walking attire. On several of these occasions my escort was E. M. Ward, not then a Royal Academician, but a young artist of whom great things were already expected. Subsequently I had the pleasure of knowing him and his beautiful and charming wife intimately, and delighted in the privilege of being admitted into his studio. I remember on one occasion his showing me a cast of the face of Mary Queen of Scots, and pointing out the great resemblance it bore to our beloved Queen. He made use of this cast in painting his "Death of Rizzio," which is surely one of his finest works, not forgetting the three or four which may perhaps be considered its peers. There is a fine touch in the "Death of Rizzio," which perhaps escapes a hurried gaze. I mean the slight bending of the flames of the candles on the table, indicating the draught from the staircase through the door by which the conspirators are entering. It is astonishing the life this little incident gives to the picture.

I believe a new school has arisen since E. M. Ward was in the height of his popularity; but it is pleasant to know that many of his works enrich our National Gallery, and to believe that while the true and pathetic in art are appreciated—and such appreciation must be looked for through all time—E. M. Ward's worth will be recognized.

Turning over some old letters lately, I came unexpectedly on one from Dinah Mulock, which recalls
vividly a particular evening at the Rosery—not one
of the open Thursdays, but a party to which guests
were specially invited. The letter bears the date
of June, 1847, at which time the writer and I lived
not far apart, and had become so intimate that we
generally met twice or thrice a week. Also we went
out together a good deal, for I was sufficiently her
senior to play the elder sister's part when my mother
was not with us. After the usual affectionate greeting, she writes—

"I have a message to you from Mrs. Hall; she
was just going to write and invite you to a party on
next Friday week, 11th of June, to meet Jenny Lind,
and I don't know whom besides, I being one of the
happy number. She asked me to tell you this, and
ask you when I saw you to-morrow. Now, dear, will
you sacrifice Mrs. Loudon, and go? For many
reasons it would be a sore disappointment to me to
miss it, for I go not without thee. Here's selfish-
ness; but I think the Mrs. L—— family might stand
over for another week, and Jenny Lind is a bird not
to be seen in every hedge. I had agreed to go to
Mrs. Loudon's with Mrs. Wills and Mr. Masson, but
I will relinquish all for the Rosery and Jenny."

The writer then proceeds to tell of an accident
which would prevent her walking for a few days, and
was the cause of her not delivering the message in

person. Of course I too "threw over" Mrs. Loudon, knowing the next Friday would do just as well, and sharing my young friend's desire to meet Jenny Lind.

I can remember many a *furore*, but never anything so warm and lasting as that which the appearance of Jenny Lind excited ; and I think it was to the honour of the English people that it was not only the rare voice of the " Swedish Nightingale " which so stirred them, but that the generous, self-denying character with which she was justly credited, combined with her artistic gifts to render her nearly angelic in their eyes. Long ago as it is, I well remember that " Jenny Lind evening " at the Rosery. The party was not a very large one. The rooms were pleasantly full, but not so crowded as I had often known them on the Thursday evenings, and I think both Dinah Mulock and I felt honoured in being invited to a very select party. I know there were several notabilities present, but I do not recollect their names. There seemed a hush of conversation for awhile, as if there were a brooding fear that the expected cynosure would disappoint its worshippers—as cynosures are a little apt to do. But no ; I do not think the Nightingale was especially late—I rather think all other guests had arrived unusually early.

At last, with a sufficiently loud voice, " Miss Lind " was announced—Miss Lind and ——, I quite forget

the chaperon's name, but she had a chaperon, I know
—and the simple-mannered, simply attired, smiling
girl advanced into the room, shaking hands with
host and hostess, and two or three other personages
known to her. Of course several introductions took
place, but Mrs. Hall had always excellent tact, and
she seemed to shield her guest from anything like
obtrusive attention. Yet, as the evening wore on,
one could see that Jenny Lind was pleased—pleased
with that childlike pleasure, the liking to be liked,
for she had not an atom of mock humility, which is
surely only an offensive form of pride. As every one
knew, she was under a deed not to sing in private,
but she looked as if she would have liked to burst
into song and delight the people who were so good
to her. She carried a charming bouquet in her hand,
not one of the formal Covent Garden Market affairs,
in which the flowers always look crowded and uncomfortable, and which would have seemed incongruous with the simplicity of Jenny Lind, but hers
was a bouquet composed of a few choice flowers tied
firmly yet lightly together with a blue ribbon—so
lightly or informally that I remember the roses
nodded. Even idol-worship must come to an end,
and Jenny Lind, the last guest to arrive, was probably the first to depart. When she was taking
leave, some adventurous admirer begged for a flower
from her bouquet ; others followed the example, till
the last blossom was bestowed, then the ribbon

dropped on the floor, and for it there was a scramble. Jenny's pale face flushed as she gave the flowers, and her beaming eyes lighted up her homely features, till she looked what I heard an artist call her, beautiful. Then with a graceful movement to the little throng about her—a movement that was half a bow and half a curtsy—she hurried away from her admirers. No doubt the simply arranged bouquet was formed from the floral offerings of the night before.

At that time I had not seen Jenny Lind on the stage ; and when I did I confess I was just a little disappointed ; not with her singing, for that was beyond all ordinary praise, but with her acting. To be sure, I only saw her once, and that was in " Lucia," a character probably too tragic for her genius. I could not but think of Grisi and Malibran, and the passions they realized by a mere gesture.

At this time Jenny Lind looked fragile and younger then six and twenty, which I believe was her age. Her health was said to be delicate, and she had the vocalist's natural dread of colds. To guard against them, she was reported to wrap up immensely in the winter. I heard an amusing account of an afternoon visit she paid when, without mentioning a carriage rug, a fur-lined cloak was left in the hall, and a shawl discarded at the drawing-room door, she remaining still warmly equipped.

Another evening at the Halls I will briefly describe for the sake of one little incident, though in

doing so I leap over nearly ten years. At this date
my dear friends occupied a many-roomed "flat" in
London, instead of the pretty Rosery ; but their
receptions were of the same character, though, alas !
many of the old faces were missing. But as stars set
on the western horizon others rise on the east ; and
so it is with the firmament of art and letters. On
the evening of which I am telling, Rosa Bonheur
was one of the guests. She had recently become
famous from the exhibition of her great picture,
"The Horse Fair," and I regarded her with immense
interest and admiration. Only about the middle
height, she yet looked so robust that one could fancy
her curbing the fiery horses she so forcibly depicts.
Very handsome, with fine dark eyes, and the short
crisp curls which were not then the feminine fashion,
her head looked somewhat like that of a man, especially as she wore a high black dress. It was evident
she was a woman who dared and determined to
despise the troublesome fripperies of ordinary
women's dress. I was seated very near the great
French painter, when Mrs. Hall brought up Sir
Edwin Landseer to introduce him to her. I could
not but be interested in the meeting of these two
famous animal-painters. The conversation was in
French, and there seemed to be on both sides
genuine gratification in seeing each other, with
mutual felicitations on their achievements. I never
heard if the acquaintance grew into intimacy and

friendship, but I am sure they must have felt much sympathy, and were both too great for jealousy to mar it. Both were supreme in showing the mentality of the animals they depicted and must have loved so well.

Few people can have been more loved and honoured than were Mr. and Mrs. S. C. Hall; and they must have felt that it was so when, in 1874, their golden wedding was celebrated. Hardworking as they had been, they were too liberal to have become rich, and the testimonial which was subscribed for them on the occasion, when sunk for a life annuity, made a very acceptable addition to their income. In being the medium for presenting it, Lord Shaftesbury spoke of them as his "august friends." The 20th of September falling on a Sunday, the golden wedding was kept on the following day. My own health was already so failing that it was something of an effort to journey from Blackheath to Kensington, but neither my husband nor I would willingly have foregone the privilege awarded us of offering our congratulations in person. It was a memorable day. I heard that twelve hundred invitations had been sent out—announcements would, perhaps, be the better word—but in September a large proportion of Londoners were of course out of town. Still, there was for many hours always a throng of well-wishers in the little house, the first comers having the grace in due order to depart as the rooms became crowded. To me, who had known the wedded pair so long and so well, the scene was very pathetic. New friends were present—but many of the old ones ; some I had not met for nearly twenty years, and who were even more advanced in age than myself, had rallied to the call.

I have spoken of Dinah Maria Mulock—subsequently the author of "John Halifax"—in connection with the Jenny Lind evening. In the winter of 1847 and the spring of 1848 we were much together, having many common friends and mutual interests. During this period she wrote several small articles for magazines, and commenced her first novel, "The Ogilvies," as the months passed on devoting herself mainly to the latter work. At this time she evinced a certain steadfastness of purpose which I admired without being strong enough to imitate. There must be plenty of people living who can remember the political excitement which prevailed in the last week of the February and the March of 1848, when Louis Philippe was hurled from his throne, and when for days at a time there was uncertainty about the fate of many distinguished personages. For my own part I could not rest or settle satisfactorily to mental employment until I had heard the latest news of the stirring events which were making history. Of course I could well remember the July days of eighteen years before, the second French Revolution as it was called, as well as hearing all my life discussed, as familiar topics, the consulate, the empire, and the restoration which had led up to that event. These memories may have warmed and intensified my interest in what was passing; still, when I knew the worst, or best of the latest intelligence, I could, to a great extent, abstract my mind from it, and settle to literary work. It was the anxiety and uncertainty which set me wondering and imagining, to the distraction of my mind.

In contrast to my weakness was Dinah Mulock's strength. She could abstain three days at a time from reading a newspaper, and when she did hear the latest intelligence she received it with apparent tranquillity. Not I am sure, that she was insensible to any sort of suffering, or ignorant of the widely spreading changes that revolution brings about, but she had determined to live mainly in the work which she was about. Besides, she was not yet quite two and twenty —too young to be a politician, though not to be a novelist. Surely her faculty of concentration was a great gift! When she consented to be my bridesmaid in the following July, her novel must have been almost completed, and her mind must at any rate have been free enough to take a most affectionate interest in my marriage.

CHAPTER IX.

Lough the sculptor—Leigh Hunt—Robert Browning—
Douglas Jerrold—Albert Smith.

IT was in the summer of 1842 that I, in company with two friends, had first the privilege of visiting Lough's studio. It has remained a never-to-be-forgotten event. I remember even the sort of day it was, not fierce and glaring, but with the sunshine slightly veiled by clouds, so that the light was steady and subdued, the very light by which to see sculpture to perfection. The works I may have occasion to mention are well before the world, but I hope some description of the sculptor himself may be acceptable. Born in 1798, John Graham Lough must have been forty-four years old at the time of which I speak, but he scarcely looked his age. Indeed I think it is a characteristic of genius, at any rate artistic genius, to wear well in this respect. A handsome man he was, about, or a little above, the middle height, with magnificent eyes that lighted up the whole countenance, and altogether a picturesque figure in his working dress of blouse and cap. As is well known, Lough was of humble though respectable origin ; but he was one of the few of what are called self-made men that in my long life I have ever known who were completely gentle-men. There was an ingrained kindliness in his nature which rendered him always courteous and con-siderate for others ; and perceiving that his visitors had some real appreciation of art, he gratified them in many ways. I do not believe mere haphazard praise would have given him the least satisfaction, rather would it have chilled him and fettered his tongue. I may observe that he spoke well, with great purity of diction, though a slight north-country burr was perceptible. He had begun the Shakespeare series some time previously, and the Ophelia and Iago were already created; and we saw the Milo—that grand statue, which, executed under so many diffi-culties, first drew attention to his power—as well as the Roman girl, and Samson, and a host of other works which helped to make his fame.

This chance visit to the studio led to my knowing Mrs. Lough, and for many years I was a frequent visitor at their house, seeing closely a great deal of their happy private life, as well as always being aware of what was going on in the studio. When the sculptor had just completed in the clay some new work, it was their habit to invite a few chosen friends to inspect it. How proud I always felt to be included ! The party generally numbered eight or ten, who met in the studio about four o'clock. Mr. Jerdan,

of the *Literary Gazette,* and other men of letters, who
professed to be art critics, came to pass their opinion
before it was too late to be of service ; and the sculptor
always listened eagerly for any suggestion, which he
was sure to weigh attentively.   Indeed, there always
seemed to me, notwithstanding his sturdy manliness,
a feminine fibre in his nature which demanded real
sympathy ; and when he perceived, by some brief
expression, that his work was understood and appreciated, his face beamed, and he showed a childlike
delight.   He was not a vain man, but of course he
knew his own power ; and it was only the praise that
had in it the ring of a true understanding of the
subject that gave him pleasure.

One of the occasions I am now describing was
when that pathetic group of the dead soldier, with
his wife and his horse leaning over him, was in the
clay.   Strange to say, the sculptor had not found for
it a name that pleased him, and he asked his friends
to help him to one if they could.   Two or three
unsatisfactory titles were proposed, but luckily the
youngest of the party suggested that it should be
called "The Two Mourners."   The name, shortened
to "The Mourners," was adopted, and by it the work
so deservedly admired has ever been known.

After revelling in the studio for an hour or two the
ladies were always invited to "take off their bonnets"
—ladies wore bonnets in those days—and we, in our
walking dresses, and the gentlemen in their morning

coats, sat down to dinner, generally as loquacious and merry a party as could be conceived. I think almost every subject under the sun was freely discussed at that table, though the dominant ones were certainly art and literature. Mr. Lough, aided by his admirable wife, was one of the most delightful hosts I ever knew, either on the occasion of one of these friendly gatherings or of a more formal dinner-party, such as they often gave. He bore his own fair share in the conversation without usurping it, and had the tact to draw forth the resources of his guests. Among his friends was the lamented Professor Forbes, who died young, and whose mind grasped science, and yet expanded to the appreciation of art.

Looking back on those days, I certainly think there was much less cynicism in conversation than is to be found now. Witty, satirical things were often enough said, and gave a zest to the "feast of reason and the flow of soul," but they were generally without malice. Honest enthusiasm was not then called "gush," and to be a "hero worshipper" was not thought "snobbish." L. E. L. was inspired to write verses on Lough's works; and the greatest of all poetesses, Mrs. Browning, has embalmed his name in her "Lady Geraldine's Courtship." Lough had the soul of a poet, which is revealed in those ideal works which are mostly in private collections. I mean such works as the Shakespeare series, or his "Milo" or "Satan." The matter-of-fact chilled him,

L

and when bound down to the real he was not at his best. It was delightful to hear him talk of Shakespeare, and Milton, and of Wordsworth, of whom he made a portrait bust. In art, he supremely revered Michael Angelo, and he spoke eloquently of his long sojourn in Rome, at a time when tourists were not "personally conducted" to the Eternal City, but when rarely any but the mentally cultivated ever visited it. The younger of their two daughters was but a few weeks old when the little family left England for Italy.

Mrs. Lough was a daughter of the late Rev. Henry North, and a woman singularly well qualified to make the sculptor happy. He appreciated her excellence to the full ; and I was told that early in their married life he let it be understood that he did not accept invitations in which his wife was not included. Consequently, when he was the guest of some noble or influential patron, Mrs. Lough was always with him. I believe there was one baronet, of great wealth, who spent from fifteen to twenty thousand pounds on Lough's works, with whom they sometimes stayed for days at a time.

But Mrs. Lough was much more than the society helpmate of her husband. Being intimately acquainted with them, I knew how completely she lifted all burthens of worldly concerns from his shoulders, leaving the man of genius to revel in his paradise of poetic and creative ideas. She even kept studio accounts, and paid weekly Lough's able assistants; and I remember hearing him say that he was not quite sure what was the rent of his house. Perhaps this was a little playful exaggeration, meant to convey the idea of his perfect trust in his wife's wisdom and goodness, and of his entire reliance on her in mundane affairs. Often and often genius is cruelly crippled just for the want of such help as she devotedly bestowed.

Mrs. Lough long survived her husband and both her daughters, reaching her four score years. In the early days of her widowhood, she presented the whole collection of her husband's original models to the city of Newcastle-on-Tyne, knowing that it had been his wish that they should be preserved in his native county. She stipulated, however, that the corporation should erect a suitable building for their reception, to be called the Lough Gallery; and it was a grief to her that up to the time of her death nothing of the sort had been done. At present— 1890—the models are exhibited in Elswick Hall, a large country house, standing in grounds which are owned by the corporation as a People's Park. Thus situated, these beautiful works are no doubt accessible to numbers of persons, but still the conditions of the gift are unfulfilled, and it is scarcely honoured as it should be.

It was at the Loughs' table that I first met a

personage whom I will call Mr. Z., and thus avoid giving pain to his children or grandchildren, if any such exist.   He was a man of considerable intellectual ability, something of a minor poet, a good conversationalist, and of gentlemanlike manners.   He was the first person I ever heard speak enthusiastically and understandingly of Tennyson.   Apparently in easy circumstances, he moved a good deal in literary society, and often entertained celebrities at his suburban residence ; his pretty wife, calm mannered but kindly, being an agreeable hostess.   No one seemed exactly to know what Mr. Z.'s occupation was, beyond the fact that it took him "into the city " every day.   I was invited to their house on one occasion, and, to make the visit more easy, was offered a bed ; thus in the after-breakfast *tête-à-tête* next morning with Mrs. Z., I had more opportunity of estimating her than I had previously had in seeing her in society.   I remember the feeling which came over me, conveying the impression that she was not a happy woman.   I think there were two or three young children ; the home was a pleasant one, and her husband seemed kind and attentive to her.   I wondered if I were right, and that some secret sorrow possessed her.   By the light of later knowledge I felt no doubt that her sorrow was vague—the apprehension of some trouble to come, without other knowledge than that they were living beyond their means.

The evening was a memorable one. It was the occasion of my first introduction to Robert Browning, then a young man ; but Leigh Hunt was the important guest, whom every one else was invited to meet.

I cannot say I had any particular admiration for Leigh Hunt, still I was curious to see a man who, for at least a generation, had been prominently before the world. I dare say I was conscious of a little prejudice against him, on account of his ingratitude to Byron ; but, if so, I hope I kept it in abeyance.

It was not a dinner party for which we assembled, but one of those sociable gatherings very common among people of letters in the early "forties." We had tea in the drawing-room, with bread and butter and cake, between six and seven o'clock, but without any attempt to render the meal what is called a " high tea." In fact, so far as I remember, that most uncomfortable meal was not then introduced. About ten o'clock we sat down to a substantial supper, which I believe was thoroughly enjoyed, for surely conversation, or even attentive listening, whets the appetite as much as bodily exercise.

Certainly there was plenty of listening that evening, for Leigh Hunt played the Sir Oracle, and harangued rather than conversed. I suppose he was considerably the eldest of the little party, mustering not more than ten or a dozen ; and he dwells in my memory as a thick-set man of nearly sixty, with fine

dark eyes and whitened hair, with his portly person
encased in a white waistcoat, which was amply
displayed by his habit of throwing back the lappets
of his coat and inserting his thumbs in the armholes
of the waistcoat.   In this attitude, and leaning back
in his chair, he discoursed to what for the most part
seemed an admiring audience.   I must confess that
he seemed to me the very type of self-satisfied,
arrogant vulgarity ; a man without reverence, and,
consequently, without the breadth of understanding
which reverence gives.   Perhaps my judgment was
at fault, and that I did not appreciate his discourse
because it was " over my head."   If so, I beg forgive-
ness of his *manes ;* yet, in later years, my opinion of
his intellectual rank was confirmed, especially when
I read that he preferred the Queen Anne writers
to the Elizabethan giants.   Such a taste seemed to
me to harmonize with the fluent pen and fluent
tongue which skimmed rapidly the surface of subjects
without ever diving to their depths.

   Robert Browning, whom years afterwards I had
the privilege to know well, spoke comparatively little
that evening ; but I was struck with the quiet dignity
of his deportment, and his expression of commanding
intelligence.   I had not then read a line of his writings,
and indeed he was new to fame.   I think his "Bells
and Pomegranates" were on the eve of publication,
or lately presented to the world.   I know he sent
me two or three numbers soon afterwards, though we

did not meet again for some time. In after years
I believe I never alluded to that evening, not knowing how intimate he might have been with Mr.
Z., and fearing the subject might possibly be
painful.

In due time the crash came, but not very noisily.
It was understood that Mr. Z., an employee in a great
house of business, had "done something" to raise
money, which would have brought him under the
lash of the law, had the lash been raised. Possibly
it was out of compassion for his gentle wife that he
was not prosecuted. The Arch Enemy, having a
latch-key to every house, had used it to tempt a man,
not without some great qualities, which backed by
conscience might have done him true service. The
temptation must have been literary ambition, the
love of congenial or superior companionship, and
the applause of the circle in which he moved. His
acquaintances were startled and grieved, but did not
seem to know what had become of him.

I am tempted to insert here one of the first letters
which I received from Robert Browning, written not
long after my introduction to him at Mr. Z.'s. It
shows how grateful the poet was for recognition in
the "forties," before he was really famous. My
reference to him occurred in an article of mine on
"Poets and Poetry," in which the author of "Festus"
was also mentioned.

"New Cross, Hatcham, Surrey,
"January 5th, 1846.

"MY DEAR MISS TOULMIN,

"Thank you very heartily for your praise—
of which I am proud—and for your kind conveyance
of it—for which I am grateful. How the class of
readers who look naturally for 'lady-like literature,"
as you say, and in place of it find your good, energetic
writing—how *they* relish the substitution, I cannot
undertake to say—but I hope with greater equanimity
than people like myself, who, having every now
and then to dip into reviews—quarterly, monthly,
weekly, and daily—never fail to detect abundant
traces of the "'prentice-hand" just discarded, I
make no doubt, from the cutting-out department of
Wellington House for bad taste and worse English—
but the difference is, happily, that whereas *you* would
infallibly warn off the coarse red paws of such fellows
from touching, even—much less writing criticism
about so delicate a matter as a "waist," long or
short—*they*, in securing such a writer as *you*, would
do far too much honour to their vaunted columns.*
Pray believe that I am very much gratified, and ever,

"Yours faithfully,

"ROBERT BROWNING."

---

* The latter part of this letter refers to the ladies' magazine, which
I then conducted, and in which my article on "Poets and Poetry"
appeared. It was a periodical that devoted some columns to the
subject of dress, but which nevertheless had several masculine and
other able contributors.

It must have been early in 1844 that I made the personal acquaintance of Douglas Jerrold. A story or two which I had offered for his *Illuminated Magazine* had been accepted, when one day, quite unexpectedly, two gentlemen visitors were announced—Mr. Jerrold and Mr. Mayhew. By the end of their half-hour's stay, a really old acquaintanceship seemed to have been established with my mother and me. It must be remembered that literary people, of whatever grade, who know each other through the pen, never do meet as strangers, and I think it was at that first interview that Jerrold, in speaking to me said, "My dear child," not that there was any rude familiarity in his manner, but only the overflowing kindliness of the veteran author to a new aspirant.

I never knew any one who had more completely two sides to his nature than Douglas Jerrold. The outside world considered him mainly as a caustic wit, a dramatist, the chief contributor to *Punch*, a man as familiar with theatrical green-rooms and newspaper offices as with his own house, and with a great deal of what is called "Bohemian" in his nature; but also he had the tenderest heart in the world, compassionating every sort of suffering, though with wrath always at white heat against selfish greed and tyranny, that brought woe upon the innocent. To me he was ever a kind friend, putting literary work of various sorts in my way. He had considerable faith in woman's capacity for intellectual pursuits, while fully recognizing the difficulties under which they laboured when struggling in the battle of life. Speaking of his magazine, he once said that he did not care how much "dimity" there was in it provided the "dimity" did not show. And to the little book called "Punch's Snapdragons," published at the Christmas of 1844, and consisting of anonymous articles and stories, there was at least one lady contributor—Mrs. White—besides myself.

It was while the Caudle Lectures were appearing in *Punch,* that one summer day my mother and I were invited to a friendly midday dinner at the Jerrolds, who were then residing in a pleasant country house at Putney.   Towards the close of the meal a packet arrived—proofs, I fancy—at any rate Douglas Jerrold opened a letter which visibly disturbed him.   "Hark at this," he said, after a little while, and then he proceeded to read a really pathetic, though not very well-expressed letter from an aggrieved matron, who appealed to him to discontinue or modify the Caudle Lectures.   She declared they were bringing discord into families, and making a multitude of women miserable.

I believe the letter to which I allude gave Douglas Jerrold great pain; and perhaps he lived to think those coarse papers unworthy of his pen. I have been told that he esteemed the "Chronicles of Clovernook" the best of his productions, except,

I suppose, his dramas, and certainly that work is eminently suggestive of deeper thoughts than shine on the surface. But looking at it fully forty years after publication, one can well understand that its philosophy was too subtle to suit the taste of the ordinary reader of *Punch*, especially when given, as of necessity it was, in detached chapters. None the less, however, was Douglas Jerrold disappointed at its reception, and I believe he finished it abruptly in consequence. He was not a vain man ; once he said he should like to spend ten years in taking in other men's thoughts, instead of giving out his own.

In my opinion Douglas Jerrold was at his best when most serious ; but then he was not always in the mood to talk seriously. I do not think he liked discussion, but rather harmonious associations. He had the reputation of a wit, but his witticisms bordered too nearly on tiresome punning to be of the first order. For example, on inquiring in society, about the year 1854, who a certain gentleman was, he was told, " Mr. Mills, from Manchester." " Indeed," he promptly replied, " why I thought all the mills had stopped there." Somehow one never remembered one thing in ten of this sort that he said, though no doubt his best *mots* got into print.

Those few hours spent at his suburban residence gave me a pleasant idea of his domestic inclinations, notwithstanding his Bohemian habits. I remember he once told me that his income sprang at a bound

from two hundred a year to two thousand, presumably from the great success of *Punch*, of which
he was one of the originators.   He always spoke
warmly of the liberality of the proprietors, who in
return had a loyal staff about them.   The weekly
"*Punch* dinners," at which things were arranged,
were strictly festivities "under the rose;" but I
remember hearing of one rather new contributor who
was suddenly dismissed because he had allowed one
of his own "good things" to transpire before it appeared in print.   Such a blow from Mr. Punch's
truncheon must have been sorely felt.   Mrs. Jerrold was
a pretty and, I should judge, a very amiable woman.
The children, I think, were most affectionately
trained, the father avowing that there were only
two faults for which he should corporeally punish
a boy—namely, telling a falsehood and cruelty to
animals.

The last time I saw Douglas Jerrold was at a
conversazione at Mrs. Loudon's, a few months or
perhaps a year before his death.   My experience in
what is called "spiritualism" had already rolled
away a cloud of difficulties from my mind, and
thrown a light on history, sacred and profane, and
on biography ancient and modern, all of which had
been obscured for generations by materialistic and
scientific teaching, unbalanced by higher knowledge.
I do not exactly remember how the subject of
spiritualism arose between us, but it was a subject

very rife in society at that time, though, generally, belief in it was treated as the craze of a few odd people, and a fit theme for ridicule. I was well accustomed to be listened to with a smile on the listener's lip and the inquiring gaze of a physician studying the physiognomy of his patient. I knew what it was to be touched on the forehead by a familiar friend, who with a shake of the head declined to hear more ; but Douglas Jerrold's behaviour was wholly different. He listened with serious and respectful attention, and when we parted—his hand, I think, being the last I shook on leaving—the last words I was ever to hear from his lips were, " I wish to God I could think as you do ! "

The following letter from Douglas Jerrold will be read with interest, especially his remarks on magazine contributions "got for nothing."

" To Miss Camilla Toulmin.

" West Lodge, Putney Common,
" October 10th, 1844.

"My dear Madam,

"I am happy to learn that you have returned recruited for your work, which I have no doubt will bear evidence of the fresh air of Devon. My engagement with the magazine ended somewhat abruptly, but I am on perfectly good terms with the proprietor, who, for a mere money-grubber, is by no means the worst of that stolid class. I feel, however, sensibly relieved by withdrawing from the work; it kept me from higher and better labour, and I was constantly trammelled by indecision and ignorance. Mr. Ingram's partner *thinks* himself literary, and will I believe edit. If I can judge correctly of his taste, it will not long survive his intelligence. He has a notion that contributions are to be got for nothing, and so they are, and when got are worth exactly what is paid for them.

"I have the satisfaction of knowing that from what has been done much good has resulted to Thorn, but almost all assistance has been from the south. Scotland has kept her purse-strings with a double knot in 'em, even though it seemed that half-farthings have been expressly issued to tempt her liberality. I will send you Thorn's book when I can pick it out of the little mountain of volumes amongst which it is at present buried.

"I shall certainly bestow my tediousness upon you the first time I come your way, and my paternal duties will, I presume, make the day not distant. We trust, also, that yourself and mamma will see us here in the great desert of Putney, in which I never breathed more freely than for months past. Now I have here the blessing of a large garden, out of which I hope to dig a book or two.

"In two or three months I hope for the pleasure of again meeting you on a work under a far different

proprietorship than that I have just quitted. With
our remembrances to Mrs. Toulmin,

"Believe me,

"Yours truly,

"DOUGLAS JERROLD.

"P.S.—I trust I need not say that at any time it
will afford me much pleasure—in so far as 'what so
poor a man as Hamlet can do'—to forward your
wishes; and therefore hope you will never hesitate
to tell me when you think I can be in the slightest
way useful."

Writing of Douglas Jerrold leads me to think of
the literary band, who for some years after the publication of the popular "Charivari," were called the
"*Punch* set." Only Douglas Jerrold and Henry
Mayhew did I know at all intimately; but I have a
few words to say about Albert Smith, who was on
the staff for some little time. Before he was much
known, I met him at the house of a widow lady, with
whose son he had been a fellow medical student in
Paris.

I afterwards met him at a dance, and so little of a
literary party was it, that probably Albert Smith and
myself were the only guests who had ever "seen
themselves in print." I was standing near the drawing-room door, where I had just been speaking to
some one, while waltzers were occupying the centre
of the room. Suddenly I perceived Albert Smith,

to whom I had not yet spoken, thread his way from the opposite side to where I stood ; in a moment his hand was on my waist, and, without a word uttered, I was whirled among the circling couples. He was an excellent waltzer, and we fell into step instantly. I enjoyed the whole thing immensely, laughing inwardly at this strange sort of "invitation to the waltz." After a few rounds the music ceased, and we fell into seats in the recess of a window, when Albert Smith broke the silence by exclaiming, " Don't you hate your fellow-creatures ? "

"Certainly not ! " I replied, with the emphasis prompted by my then state of mind, instead of some jesting retort which I might have uttered a few years later. I was under the spell of the age, when the majority of even thoughtful persons believed that we had only to educate the people to make them good, wise, and happy; when Pope's warning about a "little learning" was altogether eschewed, and when to be "the heir of all the ages, in the foremost files of time" was believed the earnest of never falling back from the onward course.

I suppose my companion must have smiled at my taking his remark so seriously, and that the conversation must have suddenly changed, for before the quadrille, following the waltz, was well formed, and in which we took no part, we were discussing German poetry, with which Albert Smith seemed well acquainted, but which I only knew through translations. He told me he had just been translating Burger's "Leonore," and said he would send me his version if I liked. Of course I was grateful, and I told him I had lately been reading a translation of that poem, which, it chanced, he had not seen, and it was arranged I should lend him the volume containing it.

The next day I received the "Leonore," printed in German, or Old English type, and found it very spirited and melodious. I remember nothing special, personally, concerning Albert Smith for some years, except the great pleasure with which I read his powerful novel, "The Marchioness de Brinvilliers," and the regret I felt that one so worthy of better things should sink to be a popular "showman." Perhaps, after all, it is well that genius should condescend. Good work is only done by those whose powers are above their labours, and do not stand as it were on tiptoe to do it. Still I venture to think that people should more nearly reach their "possibilities" than Albert Smith seemed to do.

Living out of town, after my marriage, I lost sight of Albert Smith for years. The last recollection I have of him was meeting him at a garden party. Rarely have I noticed a greater change in an individual than there was in him. By this time he was the famous exponent of Mont Blanc, who had made, or was making, his fortune fast. He had grown stout, and looked older than his age, and he

M

threw back his head with a gesture of self-satisfaction, which I had not observed in his youth. It was the period when men wore much jewellery, and he carried the fashion to an extreme. On his white (or light) waistcoat there dangled so many knick-knacks that it reminded one of a disordered jeweller's tray tilted vertically. We only exchanged a few commonplace words ; but I remember he spoke of our host's very charming suburban residence as a "pretty little box." It was a "box" where many of the *élite* among artists, and men and women of letters were often hospitably entertained ; the phrase seemed hardly gracious from one who had occupied the very modest Bloomsbury lodgings whence he sent me the "Leonore." Yet I have a kindly recollection of Albert Smith. Perhaps the poetry that undoubtedly was in his nature had not evaporated, but had sunk deep into his heart. He seemed to have a supercilious feeling that the work by which he had decided to make money was far beneath the level of his mind.

CHAPTER X.

Mrs. Somerville Wood—The Marchesa di Broglio Solari—
Bayle Bernard—Grace Aguilar—Alexis.

IT must have been before the year 1842 that I made
the acquaintance of Mrs. Somerville Wood, receiving
a general invitation to her afternoon receptions on
Sundays, and a certain week day—Tuesdays, I think.
To her evening "at homes" guests were specially
invited, and to several of them I went. I never met
Charles Dickens or any of his family at her parties,
but I have often wondered if, by any chance, she
suggested the character of Mrs. Leo Hunter. She
had, however, many amiable traits, that, so far as I
remember, are not portrayed in the novelist's famous
caricature.

I am afraid she too often confounded notoriety
with fame ; hence, in seeking to make her drawing-
room the rendezvous of celebrities, she occasionally
gathered about her a very incongruous set, so that
her house was nick-named the " Menagerie." Personages of excellent repute, and eminent in art, literature, or science, were undoubtedly her guests, but

often jostled against strange companions—especially foreigners. Exiles with mysterious antecedents she found interesting; and, being something of a latitudinarian, and a great phrenologist, she laid the faults of people very often on their unfortunate organization. I remember one evening asking a lady, who was seated near me, if she knew who a distinguished-looking man on the opposite side of the room was, and she called him a Greek count, adding, "No doubt he has committed three or four murders." A playful exaggeration, I suppose, intended to typify his character.

Mrs. Wood was the mother of a noted beauty in the early "thirties," the Honourable Mrs. Leicester Stanhope, who was subsequently Countess of Harrington. But Mrs. Stanhope was never seen at her mother's miscellaneous parties, and it was whispered that she disapproved of them. I should mention that Mrs. Wood was a gentlewoman, in many respects, of the old school, yet so receptive of new ideas that the "graft" produced great individuality of character, almost bordering, indeed, on eccentricity. Her sister, Miss Hall, resided with her in a commodious house in the Marylebone district of London, they being sisters I was told of the well-known magistrate Sir Benjamin Hall. Mrs. Wood had been twice married, her first husband, Mr. Green, having been the father of Mrs. Stanhope. Whether she was a second time a widow, or separated from her husband, seemed not

clearly understood by her mere acquaintances, Mr.
Somerville Wood's name never being mentioned.
Many persons well worth remembering were seen at
Mrs. Wood's house, and I wish especially to record
my recollections of a nonagenarian whom I met there
on Sunday, April 16th, 1843. This was the Marchesa
di Broglio Solari, and so impressed was I by the
incident that I jotted down the particulars of her
conversation within a few hours after seeing her.

She said she was ninety-five years of age, and,
indeed, she looked surprisingly old. I remember,
years afterwards, seeing in some foreign gallery a
wonderfully fine head, entitled only "Una Vecchia,"
which must have been painted from some such
original, the dents of time were so accurately marked.
Yet the marchesa appeared to have retained all her
faculties, with the exception of her hearing, to assist
which she used a small trumpet. She was descended
on her father's side from Hyde, Earl of Clarendon,
and her mother was sister to Stanislaus, last king
of Poland, who died of apoplexy at St. Petersburgh
towards the close of the last century. This venerable
lady was one of the ladies-in-waiting to the unfortunate Princess Lamballe, and she showed the scar of
a sabre wound in her hand, received in carrying a
letter from the Princess to Marie Antoinette. To
converse with the marchesa seemed like talking to
one risen from the dead. And no wonder, for her
garrulity was of the most memorable times, and of

the most undying names. She conversed, with
apparently equal fluency, in English, French, and
Italian, and quoted Latin verse with much emphasis.
I was told she also understood German ; but her
voice had the croak of extreme old age, and the
harsh intonation, which some deaf persons, though
not all, acquire.

Though *pétite*, she must have been handsome—fair
and delicate in her youth and prime ; indeed, the
activity of her mind probably prolonged her good
looks.

Though evidently very feeble physically, she talked
with energy, feeling that the half-dozen guests who
were present were deeply interested in her reminiscences.   She asked two or three persons to come and
see her portrait, painted seventy years back.   I was
not one of the favoured few, or I am sure I should
have availed myself of the invitation.   Her husband
was a Venetian noble; and she bitterly complained
that the Austrian Government allowed her only five
shillings a day after having robbed her of seven
thousand a year.   During Napoleon's Italian cam-
paign he passed twelve days in her house.   She
declared that during this time she told him truths
which he must have been unaccustomed to hear.   In
her opinion he had no vice, *except* boundless ambition
for territorial dominion !   She did not seem to weigh
very nicely all that this great exception involved.

She said Napoleon had no idea of navigation or

commerce. He talked of changing his system, and striking at the heart, instead of lopping off the limbs. By this he meant shutting up the ports of England. "At his words," she said, " I could not help smiling ; and there stood my husband in the corner, looking at me with his great black eyes, knowing well enough that I was not to be browbeaten by Buonaparte. ' Please your majesty,' said I, ' I cannot help laughing at the idea of shutting up the ports of England, when I know there is not a bit of a French wreck that can float upon the water but it falls into the lion's jaw.' Upon which he spoke to my husband, telling him I was a Caterina, and hoped I should not make him a Peter."

Then she showed the Order of the Legion of Honour which he had conferred upon her, and the orders bestowed by almost every crowned head in Europe. These she wore on her breast ; and, suspended round her neck, was a miniature of the king of Poland, with the hair of Marie Antoinette and the Princess Lamballe at the back. " It was surrounded with fine diamonds once," she said, " but my teeth have destroyed them."

Poor thing! The one-time companion of princes now lived in rather humble lodgings near Fitzroy Square.

Evidently the thoughts and opinions of the Marchesa belonged to the mental atmosphere of the eighteenth century. She insisted that the age into which she had survived was a degenerate one ; and especially was she ashamed of England, though once proud of being an Englishwoman.   I am afraid fine manners with her must have been a veneer, which age had worn away ; for, while every one treated her with a sort of affectionate deference, due to her age and condition, the contemptuous manner in which she spoke of the "present day," in a company of people who essentially belonged to it, was not exactly a sign of good breeding.   The gods of her idolatry were Burke, Fox, and Sheridan—evidently she shared Byron's opinion that Nature

> ". . . form'd but one such man
> And broke the die in moulding Sheridan."

She described with some vividness the manner in which her hand was wounded.   It was in the early days of the Revolution, when, in crossing a courtyard with a letter to the queen, she was set upon by ruffians who demanded it from her, and she must have resisted most stoutly to be so injured.   High courage and strong determination may, in extreme old age, easily harden to obstinacy of opinion and self-will. Certainly the venerable lady whom I have attempted to describe was one of the most remarkable personages now living in my memory.

Captain Bellew, an officer who had seen much service in India, was one of the agreeable persons whom I used to meet at Mrs. Wood's receptions.

He wrote a book called "Memoirs of a Griffin"—
Griffin being the nickname of a new-comer—giving
an amusing description of Anglo-Indian society at
a time when the subject had a freshness which it
cannot command now. But I mention Captain Bellew
chiefly because he declared that, having been bitten
by a mad dog, and suffering from hydrophobia, he was
cured by remedies applied by a native of India—a
native woman I think it was. He suffered from an
affection of the throat, which occasionally made his
speech difficult, and of which he spoke as the one
painful result of the terrible attack. I have heard
one or two well authenticated stories of the Hindoo
treatment of disease hardly less surprising than this
just related ; and it may be that there is still olden
knowledge to come out of the East.

It must have been at Mrs. Wood's where I first
met Bayle Bernard, the dramatist, then a handsome
man in his early prime ; though I believe I heard
him lecture a year previously. He was a good deal
sought after in society, and would occasionally entertain people with American stories. Born, and
chiefly educated at Boston, but probably of English
parentage, he could assume the Yankee twang,
convulsing people with laughter at a time when the
world was more easily amused than it is at present.
He wrote several dramas for the Irish actor, Tyrone
Power, famous in his day, and who was lost in the ill-

fated steamer, *The President*, not one survivor from the
wreck being spared to tell the tale. In my humble
opinion Bayle Bernard's best play was "The Round
of Wrong." It was not very successful on the stage,
although supported by the excellent acting of Webster
and others. In later years I knew Bernard in other
ways than by meeting him merely at parties, and
learned to respect him, not only as a man of genius,
and of varied knowledge, but as one admirable in
the private relations of life.

Bernard was a subtle and discriminating critic,
especially of that department of literature which is
known as the Belles Lettres, not, however, a cynical
one such as Byron anathematizes in his "English
Bards," but, rather, of the order which another poet,
Holmes, the American, eulogizes, thus justly applying
the following words to his friend Lowell—

> "He is the critic who is first to mark
> The star of genius when its glimmering spark
> First pricks the sky, not waiting to proclaim
> Its coming glory till it bursts in flame.
> He is the critic whose divining rod
> Tells where the waters hide beneath the sod ;
> Whom studious search through varied lore has taught
> The streams, the rills, the fountain heads of thought ;
> Who if some careless phrase, some slipshod clause,
> Crack Priscian's skull, or break Quintilian's laws,
> Points out the blunder in a kindly way,
> Nor tries his larger wisdom to display."

Bernard had a trick, which he exercised when he
knew his opinion would be acceptable, of returning
a borrowed book enriched with marginal annotations

in pencil. As for his own books, they were for the most part thickly scored.

Peace to the *manes* of Mrs. Somerville Wood, of whom after my marriage, when I ceased to live in London, I gradually lost sight. With all her eccentricities, she had a kindly nature and a cultivated mind. She was a woman of society, and, as such, at home as a hostess. Unfortunately, she carried her hatred of what she called superstition too far, so that the bolts she shot, and those which she allowed others to shoot at it, sometimes hit true religion.

Grace Aguilar is a name that deserves to be more widely known than it appears to be in the present day. Yet there must be many women, now mothers and perhaps grandmothers, who can remember the delightful books which she wrote, mainly for the young of her own sex. It is probable, too, that the generality of cultivated Jewish families treasure her memory with pride, and regret that one so gifted should have died at the early age of thirty-one.

I feel constrained to write at some length of Grace Aguilar, because—except her brothers, both some years her juniors—there can be few, if any, surviving friends who knew her as intimately as I did. Born at Hackney, in June, 1816, she was descended from one of those Spanish Jewish families who fled from persecution under Ferdinand and Isabella. In person she was not at all the typical Jewess. She had soft but expressive grey eyes, and that brown hair which only wants a touch of gold to make it almost auburn. Above the middle height, she was slender to a degree, imparting an air of fragility—with regular features, and an oval face that easily lighted up. Her voice was clear-toned, though gentle, and her manners were essentially what is understood by ladylike. She was devoted to her parents, and proud of having been entirely educated by them, save for an interval in early childhood, too brief to be worth recording. She was proud, too, of being descended from philosophers, physicians, and statesmen of Spain, although they existed under conditions, difficult to realize or wholly to excuse. In the mediæval days, when the Inquisition was a fearful power, and the Jews were so barbarously persecuted, many members of the Hebrew race, distinguished for their talents, simulated generation after generation a belief in Christianity, concealing their true faith under the strictest outward observances of Roman Catholicism. Men of this class held high offices in the State, and even in the Church.

Among the traditions associated with these Spanish Jews was a very striking one. An ancestor, I believe, of the Aguilars, holding a high position about the Court, was on his death bed, and a cardinal had been summoned to administer extreme unction and afford the last consolations of the Romish Church.

" Cease," murmured the sufferer, only about an hour

before he breathed his last, "cease your ministra-
tions. I am a Jew!" Upon which the cardinal immediately began the Hebrew prayer for the dying,
for he also was of the Hebrew race!

These pretended Christians were represented as
faithful servants to the sovereigns whom they served,
and as having amassed great wealth in the days
when Spain was the richest country in the world.
In their spacious and splendid mansions were concealed chambers in which their own form of worship
and religious observances were carried on ; and, I was
told, it was their detection in attendance on the
performance of some Jewish rite that led to the flight
of the Aguilars to England. A Spanish Jewess
of twenty-two years old was burned to death in the
market-place of Madrid, in the white satin dress
which she wore on some such occasion. It was, in fact,
a case of *sauve qui peut ;* and those of the family who
escaped owed much to the fidelity of a Christian
steward who transmitted large sums of money to the
exiles. I believe the Aguilars were merchants for
several generations, and more prosperous ones than
Grace's father appears to have been. By all accounts
he was more of a student than a man of business. He
greatly directed the historical studies of his daughter,
and would even read to her while she was engaged
with her pencil. Her "Days of Bruce" is a wonderful production for a girl of little more than twenty ;
and her romance, "The Martyr," shows how well

she was versed in Spanish history. But her literary aspirations were evident in childhood, for before she was twelve years old she composed a little drama—never published—on the subject of Gustavus Vasa. She had a wonderful memory, always recalling the salient points of books, though she was a most rapid reader—a devourer of books, as the phrase is.

Although I had a little correspondence with her previously, it was about the year 1842 that I first had the pleasure of knowing Grace Aguilar personally, and I well remember my impressions on making her acquaintance. No one could be with her for half an hour without feeling in the presence of no ordinary person. The prevailing tone of her mind was so high and so healthy that it elevated even the most ordinary topics of conversation, while the enthusiasm of her character and manner gave an additional interest to more important themes.

Although Grace Aguilar wrote simple domestic stories, such as " Home Influence " and its continuation, " The Mother's Recompense," yet she produced works of a far different class, namely, " Records of Israel," " The Women of Israel," and " The Spirit of Judaism," the last being published in Philadelphia, and edited by a learned Hebrew, Isaac Leeser. It bears the date 5602—equivalent to 1842 or 1843 A.D., from one September to the other. Of course the book is written entirely from the Jewish standpoint, but its ethics are so pure that it is a wholesome book for any reader. It justifies what was said of the author, by, I think, Mrs. S. C. Hall, that "she was a Christian in everything but name and creed."

Indeed, in remembering Grace Aguilar, I always think more of her moral elevation than of her genius ; so tender was her conscience, so charitable were her judgments, and so generous her sympathies. I call to mind two instances in which her character was illustrated. She told me that Colburn, the publisher, had proposed to her to write a history of the persecution of the Jews in England, naming a very liberal sum as requital.

" How well you will do it !" I exclaimed.

" I have declined," she replied. " We are so well treated in England now, that it would be most ungrateful to revive the memory of those half-forgotten wrongs."

And every reader of one of Chambers's *Miscellany of Tracts*, entitled, " The History of the Jews in England," which, though unacknowledged, is by Grace Aguilar, must admire the *right* spirit which prevails throughout.

Be it remembered, Grace Aguilar was by no means in easy circumstances. I am sure that at the time she refused Mr. Colburn's tempting remuneration, every guinea she earned by her pen was of consequence to her.

I think it was a little later that a circumstance

occurred which slightly increased the income of Mrs.
Aguilar and her daughter.   Upon this Grace wrote
to the editor of a magazine, to which she contributed,
and which, truth to tell, did not pay its staff
liberally, volunteering to accept half the sum which
she had been accustomed to receive for her articles,
so that there might be the little surplus for those
who wanted it more than she did.

One of the short articles from her pen, that
excited a good deal of attention, was her " Exposition
of Zanoni," which she wrote soon after the publication
of that powerful and mystical romance.   So subtle
was her explanatory analysis, that it led to acquaintance with Lord Lytton—then Sir E. L. Bulwer—
who told her that to two women, herself and Miss
Martineau, he was indebted for the truest understanding and best criticism of his work.   He mentioned
her article in the introduction to a new edition of
the book.   " Zanoni," is not the sort of production that
one expects to be grasped and appreciated by a
young woman of four or five and twenty ; but Grace
Aguilar was always at her best when dwelling on
great themes.   Every year her mind developed, and
I am inclined to think that if her life had been
prolonged, she would have written more and more
on serious subjects.

Always of a delicate constitution, and of the
sensitive temperament, which so often belongs to the
gifted, her emotions probably helped to wear her

out. However this may have been, not long after
her great sorrow, the death of her father, her friends
became anxious, though not at first exactly alarmed,
about her. But the illness which had seized her
stealthily crept on, leaving only her bright mind
unimpaired. When she was too feeble to walk or
stand without support, I saw her propped by pillows,
pen in hand, with eye as bright and manner almost
as cheerful as they ever had been. In the spring of
1847 she rallied a little, and her visit to Frankfort,
where one of her beloved brothers was studying
music, was undertaken with the intention of trying
the German baths, which had been recommended;
a confident hope being entertained that a cure would
be effected.

But her insidious malady had taken too firm a
hold, and she gradually faded away until released
from her sufferings in the autumn of 1847. When
speechless, she made known her wishes and feelings
by the finger alphabet of the deaf and dumb; and,
significant of her faith and resignation, her last
words were, "THOUGH HE SLAY ME, YET WILL
I TRUST IN HIM." Her ashes rest at Frankfort,
where she died. Life must have had many promises
of sweetness to Grace Aguilar could she have recovered health and strength. Her genius was meeting with recognition; even the usually cold and
cautious *Athenæum* praised her; she had troops of
friends, and her mind was full of literary projects,

N

which it would have been her delight to carry out. Her heart was warmed by the rising fame of her brother, the pianist and composer, many of whose beautiful compositions surely belong to the music of the future. It must be conceded that Grace Aguilar had great ambition—the desire, like that of Byron, "to live in her land's language." Ambition has been called the "last infirmity of noble minds." Is not infirmity too harsh a word ?　What great thing could ever have been done without the strong desire to succeed, and to win that recognition which deserves to be called sympathy rather than praise ? Yet, if asked the question, I am sure Grace Aguilar would have said that it was a finer thing to live a poem than to write one, all unconscious that her own nobility of soul was a fountain of poetry.

One of the half-forgotten minor poets of her day, Nicholas Michell, wrote some touching lines on her death, lines which I stumbled upon in an old magazine only the other day.　I extract a couple of verses—

> "Daughters of Judah ! mourn—from yonder shore
> 　Hear Death's low murmur'd knell ;
> The eye is closed, the heart shall beat no more
> 　Of her ye loved so well.

> "There sets the brightest star that Hebrew eyes
> 　Hailed in the heaven of mind ;
> There droops the fairest flower that worth could prize,
> 　But leaves its sweets behind."

I have spoken of Grace Aguilar's "Exposition of Zanoni," and I have sometimes fancied that Lord

Lytton's mystical romance may have been one of the
forces which gave an impetus to thought on occult
subjects towards the middle of the present century.
Of course there were always finer spirits, who combined largeness of views with reverent faith in the
mighty mysteries of the unseen world ; but, for the
most part, those who had this reverent faith hedged
themselves round with narrow verbal definitions, to
which they obstinately clung. People of this class
can never argue, they only assert, and consequently
have no influence over the persons they most desire
to convert. It is distinctly within my recollection
that, at the period to which I allude, the prevailing
tone of intellectual society was negation of the
mystical. Even people who considered themselves
Christians were of opinion that sublime mysteries,
such as Bulwer Lytton endeavoured to expound, were
but the armoury of poets and novelists.

I cannot remember the precise year, but I think
it was midway in the "forties" that I made one of
a party assembled to meet a *clairvoyant*, known as
Alexis. I was not acquainted with the hostess at
whose house the gathering was held, but a dear
friend of mine knew her slightly, and was able to
procure admission for herself and me. I remember
we each paid three-and-sixpence for this privilege ;
such subscriptions of some eighteen or twenty
persons, making up the fee necessary for the
young Frenchman. The house at which the meeting

took place was in the neighbourhood of Cavendish Square—Wimpole Street, I think—and was the residence of people of good position and high repute. I had heard that Alexis, with eyes bandaged, could describe articles, or read writing, enclosed in thick opaque coverings. As my own test, I wrote out the lines from Macbeth—

> "Can such things be,
> And overcome us like a summer cloud,
> Without our special wonder!"

enclosing them in a strong tortoise-shell card-case. When, however, I had been a little time in the front drawing-room, where the visitors were assembled, I thought my test would scarcely be a fair one; for I perceived that Alexis—a youth of apparently about eighteen or nineteen years of age—could not speak a word of English, and, consequently, in his normal state, would have difficulty in deciphering the Shakesperian quotation. I should mention that the process of bandaging the young Frenchman's eyes consisted in placing a piece of cotton wool over each closed eye, and then using three large white handkerchiefs, one in the ordinary blind-man's-buff fashion, and the others transversely across each eye; and I felt persuaded that for him to decipher a single word within my thickly lined card-case would be quite as wonderful as the reading a paragraph. Accordingly, I retreated to the little back drawing-room, which, though communicating with the front room by folding doors, was quite empty, and, seating myself in the remotest corner, removed the paper I had written, took one of my visiting cards which I was carrying loose about me, and, tearing off my name, wrote on it with my pencil the single word " Alexis." This fragment of a card I enclosed in the card-case, and returned to the front room to take my turn—which soon arrived—of testing the *clairvoyant's* power. And the following was my experience.

After giving Alexis the card-case, I never allowed my eyes to wander from it for an instant. He pressed it to his chest and, I think, to his bandaged forehead, saying as he grasped my hand, " Pensez y'en bien." This I did to the best of my ability. Then, speaking deliberately, he exclaimed, " Seule carte ; " and, while it was passing through my mind that the card was mutilated, he added, " Carte déchirée," and then, speaking more rapidly, he continued, " Seul mot—six lettres—oh, c'est moi," pushing the card-case from him in token that his task was done.

Shortly afterwards a tall, aristocratic-looking man, apparently a little past what is called middle-age, entered the room. He was evidently somewhat lame, and walked with the aid of a stick, but, withal, had an unmistakable military bearing. I did not catch his surname, but he seemed known to several persons present, who spoke of him as " the colonel." Every one seemed willing to make way for him, and he advanced to the table where Alexis was still sitting, and placed before him, what looked like, and I doubt not was, an old-fashioned fan-case. I was near enough to see and hear all that went on, though I will not trust myself to repeat—as I have done in my own case—the exact French phrases that were used. I was content with remembering their meaning.

Not only the colonel's eyes, but several other pairs of eyes were fixed unflinchingly on the faded fan-case, the contents of which Alexis was called on to describe. Perhaps the colonel—who came, I think, as a sceptic— did not obey the edict, " Pensez y'en bien," quite as earnestly as I did ; however that might be, Alexis was longer before he spoke than he had been in my case ; perhaps there was a silence of two minutes, but not more. It was broken by Alexis declaring that the fan-case contained " something white wrapped in paper whiter than itself ; " something "*piqué*," I re- member was a word used. After a little pause he proceeded, " Something taken from a living body— something taken from your body."

" It is wonderful ! " exclaimed the colonel, with an additional strong expression of surprise. Then he opened the fan-case to show what it contained. This was a fragment of bone about five inches long, in shape singularly like a miniature bayonet, and wrapped in what used to be called silver paper. The gallant colonel had been severely wounded at Waterloo, and this fragment of bone had been taken from his leg. He must have "joined the majority" long ago ; but, probably, there remains some family tradition of the circumstance I have described, and, if these pages should meet the eye of any descendant acquainted with it, it would be a service to the cause of truth to confirm my statement. The friend who was my companion kept very much to herself the particulars of her experience. But she was as fully satisfied as myself, and finding there were fresh arrivals to crowd the room, we departed without waiting to be witnesses of further marvels.

CHAPTER XI.

Mrs. Loudon—Mrs. Cowden Clarke—Louis Blanc—Sir Isambard Brunel—William and Mary Howitt—Anna Mary Howitt—Myra Drummond.

MRS. LOUDON must not be forgotten among the friends of some celebrity whom I remember with pleasure. Distinguished as a writer of fiction, she, in middle age, acquired, or, at any rate, improved, her knowledge of botany in order to be a literary helpmate to her more famous husband, who died before I knew her. The incident, however, which was said to have led to their marriage, was sufficiently amusing. I cannot say that I heard the story from her own lips, but it was so widely bruited among her older friends that I have no doubt of its truth.

About the year 1830 or 1831 a novel, entitled " The Mummy," was published anonymously, and attracted considerable attention. I remember reading it—a well-thumbed library book—at the seaside in 1834, and, though perhaps too young to enter fully into its satire, I found it very entertaining. I have never seen it since, but I know it represented the resuscitation of a royal Egyptian mummy, who is brought face to face, not with the European civilization then existing, but with what the author conjectured would be the inventions and circumstances of, I think, the twenty-second century. Few people imagined the work to be written by a woman, though it was the production of the future Mrs. Loudon, then Miss Webb. A common friend of hers and of Mr. Loudon's, hearing him praise "The Mummy," asked him if he would like to meet the author.

"Above all things," he replied.

"Then come and dine with us some day soon, and I'll try to manage it. Tell me what day would suit you, and I'll write to the novelist at once."

Thereupon a day was named which suited all parties ; and when Mr. Loudon entered his friend's drawing-room, a spinster, of about forty years, was introduced to him as the author of "The Mummy," and as the lady he was required to take down to dinner. A sympathetic friendship was soon established between the old bachelor and old maid, a friendship which ripened into an attachment that led to their union. It lasted a dozen years, and was a happy one, only marred by Mr. Loudon's ill health ; in spite of this drawback he led, as his valuable works prove, an energetic and busy literary life, aided constantly by his devoted wife.

Mrs. Loudon had been a widow for two or three years when I first knew her, and her young

daughter, her only child. The latter was as much a
" spoilt child " as a very good and clever girl could be.
She was pretty also, and so precocious that, at the
birthday party to celebrate the completion of her
fifteenth year, which took place in 1847, she appeared
and was treated as the grown-up daughter of the
house. Mrs. Loudon moved much in literary society,
and gathered many notable people about her. Her
receptions in Porchester Terrace, which were frequent
in " the season," and occasional in the winter, were
very agreeable meetings. There was very little cere-
mony and no rigid exactions of dress. Lady artists
and literary women, with but light purses, might come
in walking costume if they pleased, and trip upstairs
to take off their bonnets and make their hair tidy,
with the certainty of a welcome, as warm as if they
had stepped out of a carriage and displayed an
elaborate toilette. Tea and coffee and light refreshments during the evening were at hand, but, so far as
I remember, only on a few special occasions was an
elaborate supper provided.

I have mentioned Mrs. Loudon's interesting
daughter ; and the result of her precocious mixing so
much in animated society was that, by the time she
was seventeen, she was what is called *blasée.* A
mere evening party, or carpet-dance, such as ought to
satisfy a girl of that age, was too tame for her taste ;
she already required private theatricals or a fancy ball.
I remember seeing " The Rivals " acted in the Por-

chester Terrace drawing-room, a portion of which had been curtained off for a stage, in which I am pretty sure Agnes Loudon represented *Lydia Languish;* but the circumstance is chiefly noteworthy that I may bear my testimony to the splendid acting of Mrs. Cowden Clarke as *Mrs. Malaprop.* This was a character in which the famous Mrs. Glover was considered greatly to excel, and I recollect her impersonation of it well. Mrs. Cowden Clarke, however, gave, in my opinion, a subtler and finer interpretation of the character. Mrs. Glover emphasized the absurdities she had to utter, and seemed to share in the mirth she provoked ; Mrs. Cowden Clarke had that great histrionic gift, perfect command of her countenance, and seemed quite unconscious of her solecisms.

Later on I knew Mrs. Cowden Clarke and her clever husband very well, though, in consequence of their long residence in Genoa, our intercourse for many years was by letters only ; for twice when she was in England I missed seeing her by unlucky chances. Mrs. Cowden Clarke is, I suppose, best known from her laborious and most valuable work, the "Concordance of Shakespeare." But she worked in many other literary fields. The cleverest member of a gifted family, Mary Victoria Novello married at nineteen a man of forty, but there could not easily have been found a more well-matched pair. Both were devoted, before all else in literature, to the elucidation of Shakespeare : he by lecturing, she by the pen ; and so far did their enthusiasm carry them that their letter paper and envelopes bore the impression of the great bard's head, instead of crest or monogram.

There is a work of Mrs. Cowden Clarke's less known than I think it deserves to be ; I mean " The Girlhood of Shakespeare's Heroines," in which her vivid imagination and subtle knowledge of human nature—of character working on circumstances, and circumstances developing character, are powerfully evinced. The work consists of fifteen stories, which, if I remember rightly, were published monthly. They are paged for binding as three volumes, and are really delightful reading for those to whom Portia and Desdemona and Juliet and Helena and the rest of the group are verily real personages. The manner in which " The Thane's Daughter " is represented as the self-willed cruel child is masterly, though more pleasant is the training of the young " Heiress of Belmont " by her lawyer uncle, whom she adores, and who imbues her unconsciously with love of his own studies—but to chronicle their individual merits would be out of place here.

Agnes Loudon married a barrister, but died young. When I call to mind those pleasant evenings at Porchester Terrace, Mrs. Loudon's drawing-room seems tenanted by the presences that "come like shadows so depart." Of the throng of eminent people whom I remember—many already men-

tioned in these pages—there are now living, as far as
I can call to mind, only the great artist Tenniel, who
at a fancy ball about the year 1849, appeared in a
most picturesque mediæval costume, Mrs. Cowden
Clarke, and her sister the Countess Gigliucei, better
known as the famous Clara Novello.

Artists, authors, political personages are removed
from the world to make way for a new race, who
look upon the events of forty or fifty years ago as
ancient history. By the way, among political personages I must mention Louis Blanc, whom I met
one evening at Mrs. Loudon's. When I entered the
room, rather more than half the expected guests
had arrived, and I noticed a figure standing on the
hearthrug in conversation with two or three gentlemen. It was a pigmy of a man, in a costume so like
a shabby livery, that for an instant I took him for a
page, who had some servant's duty to perform in the
drawing-room. Soon, however, I perceived that he
was a personage who excited curiosity, though to me
he was singularly repellant. The face was that of a
middle-aged man, weather-beaten and hard in expression, while the pose of the figure was that of
arrogance and self-sufficiency. He might be intellectual and full of misdirected energy, but he looked
like one that could never be metamorphosed into a
gentleman.

Somewhat antecedent to my acquaintance with

Mrs. Loudon was the occasion of my becoming rather intimate with Sir Isambard and Lady Brunel. They were old, and I was comparatively young, but I had written something in connection with the Thames tunnel which gave them pleasure, and established a bond of sympathy, that bridged over the difference of age. Of course I had nothing to say from an engineer's point of view, but from early girlhood I had heard the feasibility of a tunnel beneath the Thames being constructed discussed with almost the acrimony of a political question, and having read the exhaustive article on the subject in Knight's "London" I was warmed to enthusiasm for the character of the man, independent of his work. Now that engineering works, so much more wonderful, have been accomplished, it is easy to speak slightingly of the Thames tunnel, but we should remember that Brunel was the pioneer of many things in mechanics, and that his untiring energy and indomitable perseverance under a succession of difficulties have rarely been equalled.

It must have been about the year 1842 that I received a brief letter from Brunel in that exquisite handwriting of his—literally like copper-plate—which has often been lauded. It was dated from the country —the seaside, I think—and expressed a wish to see me when he returned to London. Alas! the terrible paralytic stroke intervened, and the one or two letters I subsequently received were in the palsied hand of

suffering old age. Months elapsed before he was
well enough to see people, but at last I was asked to
call in Great George Street. I was met so cordially
and made so welcome that I paid several visits.
Brunel was at this time seventy-three years of age,
and his wife not many years younger. I believe I
was a good listener ; and, assured of my sympathy,
they poured out their reminiscences freely, or rather
I should say Lady Brunel did, for the old man was
not voluble, though he often, by nod of the head, or
some short exclamation, confirmed his wife's words.
She was a little old lady, with all her faculties bright
and apparently unimpaired ; he, with a ponderous
head, surmounting what might be called a thick-set
figure, bore in painful evidence the signs of the recent
stroke.

No doubt Isambard Brunel had, throughout his
long life, given abundant proofs of his commanding
intellect ; but his broad sympathy, his constancy of
heart, his warm affectionateness of nature, combined
with his stricken condition, were what to me consti-
tuted the pathos of his old age. I do not believe
that his mind was seriously impaired at the time to
which I allude, though speech seemed sometimes
difficult ; and occasionally, when mention was made
of incidents in his early life, a great bead-like tear
would roll down his cheek. The old couple usually
—I might say always—sat side by side ; often the
old man would take his wife's withered hand in his,

sometimes raising it to his lips with the restrained fervour of a respectful lover. One of his biographers has said that if he had not been a great engineer he would probably have been famous as a philanthropist ; and I can quite understand the opinion, so ready and tender was his human sympathy.

I suppose most persons know that Brunel was a French aristocrat, "under suspicion" during the Reign of Terror, and he owed his escape, under God's providence, to his skill in imitating writing ; for he copied the passport of a friend so admirably that he executed one for himself—surely, under the circumstances, an excusable forgery. He had defended the unhappy king, and addressed his dog as *citoyen*, offences which nearly brought him to the guillotine.

Brunel was at this time engaged to Miss Sophia Kingdom, a young English girl, whose acquaintance he had made when she was at school at Rouen. No doubt, when he escaped to America, he believed her to be perfectly safe on account of her nationality ; but it did not prove so. The *fiancée* of an aristocrat was not thought a safe person to be at liberty, and she was imprisoned for several months, owing her release at last to the favour of the jailer's wife. They were constant through all vicissitudes, though they did not meet for years.

These reminiscences seem cold when committed to paper, but to hear Lady Brunel tell the story of their lives, how, after the long separation, they were personally so changed that they would not have recognized each other, was full of deep pathetic interest. As a naturalized English subject, devoted to his English wife, it was not surprising that his sympathies should be largely with England. He was proud of having been knighted by the "fair young Queen" and gratified, mainly, I think, because it made his darling "my lady." But they loved to tell of the difficulties overcome in the construction of the tunnel as much as of their early romance. I am not aware if it be generally known that, for seven years, from January, 1835, to the period the tunnel was completed, Brunel never slept more than two hours at a time.

Lady Brunel herself told me of their way of life. They resided near the shaft at Rotherhithe, and, through day and night, every two hours a sample of the earth excavated was submitted to Brunel for his examination; and in accordance with its character were the written instructions given for the next two hours of work. Writing materials were always ready in his bedroom at night, and a bell was so hung as to ring near the bed. There was also a lift by which the sample of soil ascended, and by which, in return, the letter of instructions was conveyed. This broken rest was at first a great trial, but, after a while, the habit of awaking every two hours was formed, and Lady Brunel declared that for months after the completion of the tunnel she and her husband found it impossible to sleep for more than that period at a time. Nevertheless, it must have been a severe trial to a man already in the decline of life. Not merely had he to awake and then go to sleep again, but to rise and exercise his most wide-awake faculties, the life and death of his devoted workmen, and all the momentous issues of failure or success depending on the sagacity of his instructions.

It must have been in the summer of 1845 that a dear friend brought Mary Howitt to call on me. Of course, a name so long popular had been as a "household word" with me from early girlhood, and, when I heard it announced, I was enchanted at the prospect of making Mrs. Howitt's personal acquaintance. My first impression was that of mild surprise at finding the lady to whom I was introduced such an exceedingly motherly sort of personage. This feeling on my part was very foolish, for I had long survived the time when I expected authoresses, even the most famous, to be very different in their outward seeming from other women. But though, ultimately, I grew to know the Howitts exceedingly well, my original impression of Mrs. Howitt was never quite erased. On this first introduction I mentally guessed her to be the age of the year, but I believe she was a year or so older. Of medium height, and rather stout, with prominent

features, slightly projecting teeth, and hair already
grey, she would have seemed the very type of
person that younger women would have looked
up to for guidance and advice, had there not been
in her manner a certain something which failed to
command. Perhaps it was the semblance of extreme
amiability, added to the stamp of provincialism, which
I do not think she ever quite lost. In those days
railroads and cheap postage had not accomplished
their task of fusing manners, often to the detriment
of the better mannered, and "country cousins" still
existed, to be speedily recognized by their town-bred
friends.

I soon became acquainted with William Howitt,
as well as his wife, but not really intimately until
some years later, when circumstances threw us
somewhat together. Clever, worthy people they
certainly were, with a worldly shrewdness, derived
perhaps from their Quaker training, but not endowed
with that spark which constitutes genius, and dis-
tinguishes it from even the highest order of talent.
Mr. Howitt was a very agreeable man as long as
you agreed with his opinions, but he was essentially
pugnacious, and with deeply rooted prejudices. I
think his wife must have needed all her amiability
to get on with him as well as she apparently did.
Their daughter Anna Mary, who became Mrs. Alfred
Watts was, I believe, generally acknowledged to be
of a higher order of intellect than either of her

parents. When I first knew her she was somewhere between two and five and twenty, and was decidedly an attractive young woman. Fair, scarcely so tall as her mother, but delicately proportioned, with mobile features, that responded to every emotion, she revealed her artistic temperament very distinctly, whatever the topic of conversation might be. She resided for some time at Munich, for the purpose of improving herself in painting, which she studied under a great German painter. But she always preserved a manner of her own, which enabled those who recognized it to know her pictures at a glance.

Anna Mary Howitt, however, could write as well as paint, and the two volumes she published entitled, " The Art Student in Munich," are really charming reading. In 1850 she witnessed the Ammergau Passion Play, and in the work just named she describes her impression of it. It is a very able article, but perhaps too minute in its details, a fact which makes the reader's interest somewhat flag. Honestly speaking, a little brochure, by Edith Milner, not a quarter the length, descriptive of the Ober Ammergau play, as represented in 1890, seems to afford a more striking impression of it than the more elaborate exposition of the elder writer. A good deal of nonsense has been talked about the play, almost always by people who have not seen it, some declaring the representation profane, others

calling it childish and quite unworthy of this matter-
of-fact nineteenth century. It might deserve this
censure were it vulgarized by frequent representation ;
but only once in ten years is this survival of mediæval
piety and art exhibited to the world ; and the little
book of which I am speaking describes the artistic
methods by which the Great Story is set forth in
a manner that touches the heart as well as kindles
the imagination.

This, however, is a digression ; and my recollections of the Howitts would hardly be worth noting
did I not desire to give my personal testimony with
regard to a literary matter, about which there was a
"quarrel of authors" that made some sensation about
the years 1846 and 1847. Mr. Howitt was reported
to have been the mainstay, if not the originator of a
publication, called *The People's Journal*, and to have
been, in some strange way, wronged by the editor and,
I think, proprietor, Mr. Saunders, a clever man, then
little known in the literary world, but who afterwards
made his mark. That the Howitts did not originate
the work I know, because Mr. Saunders—a perfect
stranger—called on me some little time before the
first number appeared to enlist me as a contributor.
It was to be a cheap weekly journal, entertaining yet
instructive, expressive of the "liberal" progressive
ideas, which were then the order of the day. As
my home happened to be almost *en route* for Mr.
Saunders in his daily walks, he called several times

to tell me of the different authors he had engaged, and, mentioning his desire to obtain the co-operation of William and Mary Howitt, was one day full of glee when he told me he had obtained their promise to write for him. I am nearly sure that one or two, or even more numbers of the journal had appeared when this happened, and the success of these early numbers filled him with hope for the future.

In due time articles by William and Mary Howitt appeared—and shortly afterwards I heard that Mr. Howitt had put money into the concern, so becoming virtually, if not actually, a partner. This position appeared to give him some authority, which he exercised by flooding the work with his own and his wife's contributions. It would hardly be a figure of speech to say that, when Mr. Saunders told me how the work was going down, he almost tore his hair with vexation, attributing it entirely to the Howitt mismanagement. The quarrel soon became a disastrous one for all parties concerned. The Howitts seceded, and set up a journal which they called *Howitt's Journal,* and which proved very short lived. But the division injured the *People's Journal;* and the Howitts being better known than John Saunders, their losses were more commiserated than his ; but I was enough behind the scenes to feel deeply for the originator of a work which promised so fairly until marred in the manner described. The *People's Journal* struggled on for a few months, some

of the contributors—my humble self among the
number, consenting to write at a lower rate of remuneration out of sympathy with the founder's trials.
I think Mr. Saunders behaved with more dignity and
courtesy than did Mr. Howitt, for the latter made it
understood that those who continued to write for the
People's Journal, could not be accepted as contributors to his new venture. I confess I never regretted my fealty to the "old ship," though it made a
little coolness with the Howitts for a time. I have
never seen John Saunders since those days of strife
and struggle; if alive he must be a very old man,
but he was greatly misapprehended in the affair to
which I refer, and I feel it a duty to state what I
know on the subject.

It was about the time of my association with the
People's Journal that I became acquainted with Myra
Drummond, a young artist who certainly deserved a
wider popularity than she ever attained. I met her
at dinner at the house of an old friend—and we, with
host and hostess, made up a party *carré.* The half
hour before dinner is a much maligned period of
time; it has so often been pronounced dull and flat,
when people are supposed incapable of animated
conversation, that what is very frequently a falsehood
is accepted as a fact. It is one thing to have a
pleasant appetite for the principal meal of the day—
another to come to it like a surly, ravening wolf.

Our host was Octavian Blewitt, for some forty years the secretary of the Royal Literary Fund, and I have known but few better-read men, or men more rich in anecdotal remembrances than he; and his conversation alone would always prevent a small party being dull. Myra Drummond sat with her back to the window in the waning light of late autumn or early spring, I forget which it was, and the indistinct view I had of her face did not impress me greatly. In fact I at first thought her a little commonplace looking. Moreover she was rather an observer than a talker, as painters often are, and for a time she joined but little in the conversation. But at dinner I sat opposite to her, and soon saw how the pale and rather sallow face lighted up, and the bright eyes beamed with intelligence. I noticed, too, that though slightly deformed, she was not ungraceful; and that, though not a great talker, all she said was worth hearing. Before the evening was over I found myself admiring her greatly, and hoping that we might become friends.

Myra Drummond was the painter of a beautiful picture that, through the engravings of it, was well known at the time of which I am speaking, and must, indeed, be familiar to many people still. I allude to the portrait of Helen Faucit—now Lady Martin—in the character of "Pauline" in the *Lady of Lyons*. This great actress embodied Bulwer Lytton's creation in a manner never to be forgotten by those who witnessed it, as I did three times during the first month of its production—only to find new beauties on repetition. Undoubtedly the *Lady of Lyons* is a great play, without ranking among the greatest that dramatists have produced; and the actors in it, notably Helen Faucit and Macready, so rose to the occasion that they expanded every ideal, and must have delighted the author of the play. Myra Drummond's picture was not only a life-like, life-sized portrait of the actress, but it presented her absolutely as Pauline Deschappelles. The moment chosen for delineation is one of the most exciting in the play—that in the last act, where Pauline is receiving congratulations on her approaching divorce, and is told that she ought now to be excessively happy. In the depth of anguish she only ejaculates the word "Happy!" Into that one word the great actress threw the expression of her misery, whilst her look responded to her emotion; and this the artist studied night after night at the theatre until she was able to produce it on her canvas.

The artist who could paint that picture might well be credited with exceptional power.

My acquaintance with Myra Drummond was but too brief. We exchanged friendly visits, and became somewhat confidential, for there were many points of sympathy between us; but marriage came to us both about a year after our meeting, and altered the conditions of our lives. I ceased to live in London, and the circumstances of her marriage form a pathetic story which I have to tell.

I remember calling on her one day, after we had grown rather intimate, when she told me of a picture she was painting—though without offering to show it me—a Roman subject, which she said had been delayed from the difficulty in finding a suitable pair of legs from which to paint ; but she added that her brother had at last discovered a life-guardsman, who exactly answered the purpose of a model for her Roman soldier. We were in her studio on a first floor, in one of the streets off the Tottenham Court Road, then rather a favourite resort of artists, and the middle window had the glass carried up to the ceiling in the manner requisite to arrange the light. I suspect—though I do not positively know—that the apartment, with all the usual litter of easels, unframed and half finished works, and odd objects that have their uses, was the young artist's living-room as well as her studio. She did not conceal from me her poverty, which, indeed, was " writ large " everywhere, but I think she had the sort of pride which would have made her reticent on the subject with any wealthy acquaintances. I, too, for years had been compelled to put Pegasus in harness to draw the bread cart, and could understand her struggles and her trials.

There has been a great deal of noisy rejoicing that

the days of "patronage" are over; but if ever there was a case where a powerful patron was needed, it was in that of the rather reserved Myra Drummond, who was too proud to be her own trumpeter, or to make advances in society, she requiring rather to be drawn out. I remember her repeating to me an axiom of her father's, which I have never forgotten, "Keep true to your art, and it will be true to you." But the question often arises whether the exercise of a little worldly wisdom may not in the long run prove fidelity to art. "Put money in thy purse," even if it must be by drudgery, is often good advice to the young author or artist; for, without a certain amount of ease and independence, great intellectual work has very rarely been done; so rarely, indeed, that the exceptional instances of it are only delusive. That multitude of entities called "the public," which is supposed to supersede and to be a great improvement on the individual patron, is most gregarious, acting almost always on the "follow my leader" principle. How often does it happen that if praise of a book is elicited, the commendation—provided the work is not already famous—is qualified by the observation, "But then, you know, I don't pretend to be a critic!" Or, if a picture becomes famous some time after its exhibition, something of the same sort is said. "Oh yes, I remember it very well. I thought it beautiful; but I didn't say anything about it because I know I am not a judge of pictures." If these poor timid souls had but the courage to band together and make a reputation, then indeed might the public be said to worthily supersede the patron.

It must have been a little later than the visit I have described, that I heard more of the handsome life-guardsman, who, I fancy, served for other subjects besides the Roman soldier. In hours off duty he also carried Myra Drummond's paintings to the picture dealer's for sale, with instructions, I am afraid, to take almost anything that was offered for them. I remember she considered he had a real appreciation and love of art, and had been of the greatest service to her. And—the next thing I heard, was that they were married! How the news reached me I do not precisely remember, probably through a message, or some correspondence between us, or I should not otherwise, after my own marriage, have journeyed from Blackheath to Albany Street, Regent's Park, to call on the artist.

This visit was about two or three months before the birth of her first child. Her husband was still in the ranks; and apartments in Albany Street had been chosen on account of their proximity to the barracks. She seemed glad to see me, and spoke very freely of the step she had taken, and, certainly, without regret. Of course I made the best of her position, and I remember saying something to the effect that many a gentleman, in a fit of temper or distress, or from incapacity in other

way to enter the army, had enlisted as a private
soldier. And she retorted, "My husband was not
a gentleman; he is one of five sons, peasant-born."
And I am nearly sure she added, "they are all in
the army." The old pride was quite as rampant as
ever. There was the old look also in her eyes, that
look which poor L. E. L. described as being "heavy
with the weight of unshed tears;" and yet this look
was a little less marked than it had been in former
times. She seemed thoroughly aware that a woman
could not raise her husband's social position, though
a duke might raise any virtuous girl to his own.
This was the last time I saw Myra Drummond, now
Mrs. Pointer. I forget if it was from herself I heard
that one of the officers in her husband's regiment
had known her father, and gave her some portrait-
painting commissions.

The next thing I heard was that Mr. Pointer had
left the army, and, in conjunction with his wife,
had taken up photography and settled at Brighton.
At Brighton, I believe, the artist died, to be followed
to the grave in a few months by the husband, who,
it was said, loved her so well that he died literally
of grief for her loss.

In the summer of 1848 I married, and Camilla
Toulmin merged into the name which the title-page
of this book bears. The future chapters will recall
the recollections of Camilla Crosland.

CHAPTER XII.

American friends and acquaintances—Charlotte Cushman—Bayard
Taylor—Nathaniel Hawthorne—Mrs. Beecher Stowe—Madame
Le Vert—Grace Greenwood—Messrs. Ticknor and Fields—
Margaret Fuller.

IT was after my marriage that various circumstances
made me acquainted with several Americans of note.
I had met Charlotte Cushman in society previously,
but learned later to really appreciate her worth and
her talents. I had but little personal experience of
her as an actress, for "Viola" was the only part in
which I saw her ; and it certainly was one singularly
unsuited to her, though, of course, she embodied that
creation with feeling and skill.   But I believe—
relying on the opinion of excellent judges—that
she was essentially a great melodramatic and tragic
actress.   I confess I should like to have seen her in
Romeo, in which she appeared, with her sister as
"Juliet." I wonder, when she did this, if she entertained
something of the opinion I once heard expressed by
another clever woman, namely, "that a woman of
genius would never be satisfied with a lover until
another woman of genius changed her sex and fell

in love with her." There may be a grain of truth in these somewhat bitter words—but only a grain, for, though the lofty ideal of genius may never in life be precisely realized, it may on some sides be surpassed, if on others not reached. The metamorphosed woman would make but a sorry lover; for, as Tennyson finely says, that in "true marriage"—

> " . . . each fulfils
> Defect in each "

until they grow—

> " The two-cell'd heart beating with one stroke
> Life."

This is a digression, suggested by the idea of an accomplished actress depicting one of the most ardent and love-stricken characters that dramatist ever created.

But it is of Charlotte Cushman in her private life that I would speak more fully. Most people were aware that in early life she was gifted with a magnificent voice, which had been cultivated with the view of her appearing on the lyric stage; but, in some illness, she entirely lost her power as a vocalist, and had to abandon all idea of being an opera singer. Yet, happily, her speaking voice, somewhat deep-toned, if I remember rightly, remained to carry her through a successful career as an actress. She was a delightful companion, with something sensible to say on nearly every subject that could be started. Her manners

were remarkably easy and unaffected, with very little
of, what we are accustomed to call, the American
about her. To hear her read fine poetry was a real
treat, and a lesson in elocution to such as could
profit by it. One day, when she lived in Bolton
Row, we made a rather late afternoon call, and, as
it chanced that everybody had taken a midday
meal, we lingered on till the gloaming of a summer
evening. Emma Stebbing, an American sculptress,
whose acquaintance I had made in Rome, and who
died before her gifts were fully developed, was a
guest ; and, I rather fancy, it was she who solicited
Miss Cushman to read something of Wordsworth's,
to which, in conversation, allusion had been made.
The time seemed winged, listening to her, and she
appeared delighted to give her friends so much
pleasure. I remember, too, the fresh bond of
sympathy I felt in her warm appreciation of one or
two of Mrs. Browning's least-known poems.

But Charlotte Cushman was more than a woman
of genius. She bore her own trials bravely, was
generous and magnanimous in a marked degree, and
also pitifully forgiving to the ungrateful.

Perhaps to the young of the present day the name
of Charlotte Cushman is scarcely known ; but a
preceding generation will recall her, not only as a
favourite and an accomplished actress in a few special
characters, but as an ever-welcome addition to literary
and artistic gatherings.

Another of my pleasant recollections of American friends is that of Bayard Taylor. About the year 1853 we met him at the house of the late Mr. Francis Bennoch, at that time somewhat of a city magnate, who had been the friend and benefactor of the painter Haydon, and who always chose for his guests people of worth and talent. He had travelled in the United States, making many acquaintances there—hence his house was often a rendezvous of eminent Americans who came to London.

Bayard Taylor was at this period a bird of passage, on his way to other countries, and we did not see very much of him, though he spent an evening with us. But there are people whom you may like much, and know to a considerable extent very quickly; and Bayard Taylor was I think one of these. He was quite a young man—not out of the "twenties" I am sure—and full of that hopeful enthusiasm and energy which are so becoming at that age. He had already travelled much, and was planning further daring adventures. There was such an undercurrent of courage and chivalry about him that I have often thought how well suited to him was his Christian name. Not, however, till he sent me from America his volume, "The Orient," did I know how true a poet he was, and I suppose no one foresaw in him the skilful diplomatist he was destined to become. Though we had not heard from him for years, his death was a real regret to us; but how hard it is to

P

keep up a correspondence with many whom one greatly regards, only those who wield busy pens can really know. In his youth Bayard Taylor was decidedly handsome, with a glow in his complexion which reminded one of his neighbours the Red Indians. He was tall and slim, with every limb expressive of agility. Gifted and accomplished as he then was, he must have had an essentially developing mind. His fine translation of Goethe's "Faust," on which he spent several years, was produced in his later life, and evinces not only patient and artistic industry, but a maturity of genius which grasped that of the great German, in a manner which perhaps no other translator of that immortal drama. has done.

I suppose there are few English readers of fiction, having a taste for better things than the merely sensational novel, who are not acquainted with "The Scarlet Letter," "The House of the Seven Gables," and other works of Nathaniel Hawthorne, though I am afraid they are now less read—and, may I add, appreciated—than they were thirty years ago. Perhaps there is a reason for this ; Hawthorne's works remind us of the laborious, patient, and delicate art of the fine gem-cutter, and to "taste" them thoroughly every detail has to be noticed and dwelt upon, and its suggestiveness remembered. A writer who produces this sort of work cannot be extremely voluminous,

and, nowadays, for an author to retain his popularity
he must be constantly producing some new thing—
constantly, as it were, keeping himself " in evidence."
And to die, what is called prematurely, is for such an
author's grasp on the public to be to some extent
relaxed. But I desire to speak of Nathaniel Hawthorne as I remember him about 1854, rather than
presume to be his critic.

In society he was one of the most painfully shy
men I ever knew. I never had the privilege of
an unbroken *tête-à-tête* with him, and am under the
impression that with a single listener he must have
been a very interesting talker ; but in the small social
circle in which I first met him—it was at the house
of Mr. Bennoch to whom I have before alluded—it
really seemed impossible to draw him out. We were
only five or six intimate friends, sitting round the fire,
and with a host remarkable for his geniality and tact ;
but Hawthorne fidgeted on the sofa, seemed really to
have little to say, and almost resented the homage
that was paid him. Though I say this, my reverence
for him and admiration of his genius remain unchanged, for the true man is in his works—there he
reveals himself as the deep thinker, the true philo-
sopher, the charitable sympathizer with his fellow-
creatures—in short, the prose-poet.

Hawthorne's early struggles had been great, and
the recognition of his genius was slow ; probably it
was the false position in which he was so long held

down that made reticence and a shrinking shyness a
habit. Hardly anything perhaps is more at enmity
with ease of manner than the consciousness of a false
position. Still we got on sufficiently well for him to
do us the favour of meeting a few friends one evening
at our house. Really, I scarcely felt that Hawthorne
was a stranger, for I had written a review of " The
Scarlet Letter," which I understood pleased him, and
had seen a letter of his to a common friend, in
which he said some gracious things about a little
book of mine, reprinted by his American publishers ;
but neither of these little incidents was named
between us.

At the time of which I am writing, Nathaniel
Hawthorne was in the mid-prime of life, a stalwart
man whose appearance is well represented by photo-
graphs, and, if I remember rightly, by a lifelike bust.
His blue eyes, rather small for the size of his head,
had a peculiarly soft expression.

The evening he spent at our little cottage was
memorable for one amusing incident. Having perceived Hawthorne's sensitive nature, we carefully
abstained from making him the "lion" of our little
party, so that his name was not floated about the
room ; but my husband soon perceived him in earnest
conversation with his old friend, Philip James Bailey,
the author of " Festus," never doubting that they were
mutually pleased to meet each other, for " Festus,"
that mine of subtle thought, of bright imaginings and

dazzling fancies, was even better known in America than in England. Quite true it was that they enjoyed each other's society, but not till later in the evening did either of them know the other's name. Though a dozen people were chattering round about them, I think it was just the sort of *tête-à-tête* in which both men would shine. Happily our valued friend, the author of "Festus" still survives, and therefore cannot be counted among the "lights" that "are fled" of whom I am telling.

Surely Lowell, in his clever "Fable for the Critics," has summed up Hawthorne's attributes most admirably when he says—

> "There is Hawthorne with genius so shrinking and rare
> That you hardly at first see the strength that is there;
>
> *　　*　　*　　*　　*　　*　　*
>
> When Nature was shaping him clay was not granted
> For making so full-sized a man as she wanted,
> So, to fill out her model, a little she spared
> From some finer grained stuff for a woman prepared,
> And she could not have hit a more excellent plan
> For making him fully and perfectly man."

When Mrs. Beecher Stowe visited London soon after the great success of "Uncle Tom's Cabin," I was taken to an afternoon reception given in her honour. I am ashamed to say I forget the name of her host, but I have an impression that he was a dissenting minister of some celebrity. It was certainly in the early "fifties," I think in 1852 or 1853; and perhaps few authors ever received more genuine homage, during a brief stay in England, than did the little woman on the sofa to whom we were in turn introduced. I did not actually hear the words from her lips, but they were buzzed about the room as having just been uttered by her, that she "felt like a child who had set fire to a packet of gunpowder." Notwithstanding the strong Yankee twang of her dialect, there was a very charming simplicity of manner about Mrs. Beecher Stowe. She did not ignore the fact that she had done an important piece of work in the world, but showed neither mock humility nor self-laudation on the subject. I suppose she was under forty years of age at the time of which I am speaking, but her skin looked dry and withered as if by a settled tan. Her countenance was distinctly intelligent, yet I can fancy certain commonplace people ranking her as one of themselves, and rather wondering how she could have written such a book. I mean those people who seem to fancy that authors are always attired in their "foolscap uniform," much as little children imagine that kings and queens always wear crowns. But more expressive, to my mind, than her countenance, were Mrs. Stowe's hands, which, for the most part, lay very quietly in her lap. I noticed there was no wedding-ring. Small, brown, and thin, the gnarling of the joints revealed the energy of character that usually accompanies such hands. Though by no means so "spirit small" as Mrs.

Browning's hands, they had something of the same character.

Unless Byron was right in saying that Cervantes in "Don Quixote" "laughed Spain's chivalry away," I suppose no single work of fiction had such national consequences as "Uncle Tom's Cabin." It focussed the horrors of slavery ; it strengthened the hands of the already earnest active abolitionists ; it roused the lukewarm to fervour, and, no doubt, converted many opponents of the great cause, unless they were swathed in the crippling, blinding bandages of personal interest.

As is well known, the Duke and Duchess of Sutherland were greatly interested in Mrs. Beecher Stowe, "taking her up," as it was said, warmly, and when, many years after meeting the famous American, I was conducted over Trentham, I noticed that a bust of Mrs. Stowe was established in a place of high honour, namely, at the end of the long corridor, out of which opened the bed-chambers of the family. About the same time I heard a characteristic story. My informant had it from a gentleman who was a fellow guest at the table. Mrs. Stowe was being entertained at one of the ducal residences, and the occasion was a large dinner-party. In a momentary lull of conversation, Mrs. Stowe, who had been gazing somewhat earnestly at her hostess, exclaimed in a voice that every one could hear—

" Duchess, how ever do you fix your hair ? "

"You must ask Louise," replied the Duchess of Sutherland, with a smile that in no way betrayed astonishment or rebuked her guest.

In glancing at the "eccentricity" of manners of a past generation of Americans, it is only fair to acknowledge how vastly they have improved of late years. Keen observers, quick to learn, and frank in acknowledging their shortcomings—when once they realize them—they have profited by their opportunities of culture and travel. Of course they hug their prejudices still ; but the class distinction of their upper ten thousand becomes more and more pronounced ; and the reign of our beloved queen has done much to make not a few of them believe that there may be some advantages in royalty after all.

I have just been telling of the famous abolitionist writer, and now I have to mention a slave-owning lady, who brought letters of introduction to us about the same time that I was introduced to Mrs. Beecher Stowe, and who I suppose might fairly be considered typical of her class. Madame Walton Le Vert was the wife of a physician practising in Mobile, but she came to Europe under the escort of her father, Colonel Walton, who had been governor, I think, of Florida, bringing with her a young daughter of sixteen. She was spoken of as the Queen of Mobile, and was, I believe, considered the leader of fashion and the first personage there. Her entertainments,

often in the nature of garden parties, sometimes
numbered a thousand guests, and, by all accounts,
lavish hospitality in various directions was the order
of the day. I have no doubt that she felt her
wealth was as secure as if it were in the English Funds,
without any foreshadowing of the revolution that a
few years would bring about. She was a woman of
culture, and an accomplished linguist. She sought
eagerly to make the most of her time and opportunities, and as she had formed a warm and intimate friendship with the Lady Emmeline Stuart Wortley, during
that lady's stay in the United States, had, I believe,
many introductions that led her into the best London
society. Appreciating all sorts of talent, and eager
for all sorts of information, she was ready to dis-
cuss any subject, not shirking even the "domestic
institution," as slavery was called. She defended
it to a certain degree, but assuredly not wildly and
enthusiastically. I remember her saying that many
of her "servants" were descended from those who
had been in the Walton family two hundred years
ago, but that she did not desire to possess any more
of "that description of property." She insisted on
the slaves being generally attached to their owners,
and being happy, and cited her own maid—Betsy,
I think she called her—who at that moment was left
at the hotel with the key of her dressing-case in
which were four hundred pounds in notes and
gold.

She did not, however, say, what I heard some years later from excellent authority, that Betsy was Madame Le Vert's half sister, "given" to her by her father, because he thought she would prove a kinder mistress than his wife had been. Yes, it was well for Mrs. Stowe to write her second story "Dred," to show how the canker of slavery corrupted the "owners" even more than their victims.

It happened that we had the opportunity of procuring invitations for Madame Le Vert and her father to a *soirée* at the Mansion House, the object of the Lord Mayor being to gather together those who were distinguished in literature and art, and many personages of high rank who liked to mix in such society. Our American friends accompanied us, and I took the arm of Colonel Walton, as we moved about, looking out for friends and acquaintances. Rarely, however, have I felt so humiliated as I was by the deportment of this some time governor of a state—this haughty, self-sufficient slave-owner, who thought himself the equal of any peer in the room, but who from time to time relieved his cough in that American mode which Mrs. Trollope characterized as disgusting. Nearly forty years have passed since then, and I do not suppose such filthy vulgarity could be perpetrated now ; but I felt pained and ashamed beyond description at our having been the introducer of one who seemed to disgrace us, as well as himself. The better class, in a country that is really civilized,

have a certain respect for the servants who wait upon
them and clean after them, the want of which is always
taken as a sign of gross vulgarity ; but slavery was
a vice that tainted the whole nature, and corrupted
manners as well as morals, which, after all, interlace
each other rather closely.

Poor Madame Le Vert ! Affluent in circumstances,
and rich in friends when I first knew her, she little
dreamed of the change that was in store for her. Up
to the time of the American civil war we corresponded occasionally ; and when the war broke out I
was instructed to direct to her under cover to one
of the seceding generals. But the blockade interfered, and my last letter or two could never have
reached her. Then she ceased to write, for the great
trouble was upon her. I believe father and husband
died within a few years ; and she, who had been
accustomed to daily luxuries, as if they were daily
necessaries, she, whom Lady Emmeline Stuart
Wortley had apostrophized in a very touching poem
as the "chosen sister of her soul," had to face
the world, seeking to maintain herself and her
daughter; for the emancipation of the slaves swept
away her wealth. Yet she was a brave little woman,
mentally cultivated and accomplished, and had
travelled much ; so she set herself to prepare and
deliver lectures on places she had visited and people
she had known. Friends took tickets and helped
her as they were able, but I heard that her success

was not great, and that she and her daughter died really in poverty.

Though, in these pages, I purposely avoid any but the most incidental notice of living personages, I cannot close my chapter on American friends and acquaintances without some mention of Mrs. Lippincott, the lady who writes under the *nom de plume* of Grace Greenwood.   When first I knew her, some five and thirty years ago or more, she was enchanted with the "old country."   I remember one 4th of July, an allusion having been made to the day always kept as a festival in the United States, she exclaimed, "Oh, I don't want to be reminded of the 4th of July while I am in England."   But I think that young enthusiasm for much that fascinated her has faded away, and that she is now American and republican to her fingers' ends.   I feel for her affection and respect, notwithstanding some differences of opinion, and look upon her as a woman of genius whose varied talents have been too much diffused. She has written charming stories and poems, and would have made her mark as an actress, I am sure. But I suppose her speciality is that of a journalist; for, always on her visits to Europe, she appeared engaged in writing letters for American newspapers. No doubt many people grow used to the "outer" life of the journalist; but to visit places with the object of writing about them, to read books with the

intention of criticizing them, and to mix in society
with a view to describing it cannot be the way to
really enrich the mind or develop its best possibilities. Good literary work is very rarely executed
speedily.

Among the American acquaintances I made in
"the fifties" were Messrs. Ticknor and Fields, the
Boston publishers, eminent among their class as
honourable men who paid English authors for re-
printing their works, as I know by personal experience, at a period when there was no law to
prevent their appropriation of such works, and the
system of forwarding early sheets was not established.
I mention them, however, chiefly in connection with
a little incident, the memory of which recalls a far-
off time. It was early in June, in the year 1852,
the very last year of the Great Duke's life, that
Mr. Fields expressed an ardent desire to witness the
preparations at Apsley House for the Waterloo
banquet, which, ever since the battle which gave it
the name, had taken place on the 18th of June. The
guests were exclusively officers who had served in the
famous contest. Annually, from my early childhood,
I had been accustomed to hear of the Waterloo
banquet as one of the events of the London season ;
and, I believe, for some years it was not very difficult,
by application to the duke, to obtain tickets to see the
preparations, the tables laid out with rich memorial

plate and china, and, I think, faded banners raised aloft. By all accounts it was a soul-stirring sight, kindling the patriotism of English men and women, and remaining a lifelong memory. Mr. Fields had probably heard of the banquet from many mouths, but I think I fanned the flame of his desire a little, and that I volunteered to write a request for admission to the duke himself; at any rate, I was deputed to do so. Almost by return of post came a reply in the well-known handwriting, that was perfectly legible, though betraying the trembling hand of age. Three sides of notepaper it covered; but it proved to be a lithograph, so good that for two days it was undetected, my name and the date alone being added by the pen. It was a most courteous refusal, but showed that applications, like mine, were too numerous to be treated in any other way. Mr. Fields took possession of the letter, considering it "almost" an autograph; but I remember one phrase in it was "respect for his servants," being among the reasons that he could not comply with my request.

This is a trifling incident to record, but I think it shows the high-bred courtesy of the great commander, and the kindly nature of one who is reported never to have left a letter unanswered. Amid all the gala festivity of the annually recurring 18th of June, ever the minor chord of sadness must have been struck, as the circle narrowed and the vacant chairs were increased!

Writing somewhat chronologically, I ought, perhaps, sooner to have mentioned Margaret Fuller, whom I met at Dr. Westland Marston's some years previous to the time when I became acquainted with other American celebrities. She was, without doubt, a remarkable woman, whose memory is still fondly cherished in the United States, and whose name, at any rate, must be familiar to a good many English people. Several memoirs of her have been written ; and from them we gather that she was a student of Latin and Greek at an age when little girls are usually devoted to dolls ; but she loved learning, though there was much in the severity of her early training which might have worn out her taste for it. The best thing for a clever child is to mix habitually with very superior people, and this advantage Margaret Fuller does not appear to have enjoyed. Had she been early brought into contact with great minds she must have placed her own intellect in comparison with them, instead of measuring it by mediocrities, and consequently arriving at a point of self-esteem, which was sometimes rather harshly judged. It is in the nature of a paradox, and yet a truth, to say that had she learned less she would have known more. It was evident that, in early life she gave herself no time for the "crooning" which is so necessary for deep, clear thought, and for the production of great original work.

As Margaret Fuller was born in 1810, she must

have been upwards of thirty when her darling wish of visiting Europe was realized. Her reputation had long preceded her as one of the most gifted women America had yet produced. She was known to be a linguist, a journalist, a teacher of classes somewhat in the fashion of a lecturer, amalgamating in her mind science, art, and general literature in a surprising manner. Also, she was said to have the highest estimate of her own powers, which she evinced by a persistent egotism. People were curious to see her; though, perhaps, somewhat prejudiced against her, for excessive self-consciousness, even in the most eminent, is apt to provoke ridicule. I had never heard her personal appearance described, and it rather took me by surprise. When I entered the drawing-room, several, but not all, of the expected guests had arrived. The party was not planned to be a large one, and I saw at a glance who was the cynosure of the evening. A lady of medium height and size, and of graceful figure, was leaning back in an easy-chair, and alternately listening with interest, or talking with animation to the group around her, the American twang in her voice betraying her nationality. Her light hair was simply arranged, and her cheeks showed the fading, so often noticed in her country-women when the thirtieth year is passed, yet without exactly ageing the face. The outline of her head was fine, and her blue eyes beamed with candour and intelligence. She wore a dress of lilac silk, enriched with a good deal of black lace drapery. In a few minutes I found myself seated by her side, and very soon any prejudice which I might have entertained against the "strong-minded" woman ebbed away. Though egotistic, certainly, she was wise, genial, and womanly, and when I shook hands with her at parting it was with the hope of seeing her again. But an accident prevented my acceptance of an invitation which she sent me, and her stay in London was nearly over. Little could any one have conjectured the stirring scenes which she was to witness in the few remaining years of her life; scenes which taught her more of the realities of human life than all her books could have done, and brought into high relief the noblest qualities of her nature.

How she visited Paris, and some of the chief cities of Italy, lingering especially in Rome, "the city of her soul," has been described in many a memoir. It was in Rome, in the spring of 1847, that she met the young Marchese Ossoli, and it was in December of that year that, after much persuasion, she became his wife. The marriage was for a long time kept secret, for he belonged to an old patrician family of *ultra*-conservative opinions, and had it been known that he had imbibed liberal ideas from a Protestant wife, very painful complications must have ensued. Besides this, though noble, Ossoli was comparatively poor, and Margaret Fuller was a "brain worker," mainly supporting

Q

herself, I believe, by the letters she sent to American journals.

The revolutionary days which have made history were now approaching. Madame Ossoli was shut up in Rome during the siege, when she played the part of hospital nurse with unflagging devotion. She was by this time a mother, and was riven by anxieties for the little Angelo. Nevertheless, her pen was busy, and, probably, had her history of the stirring scenes she witnessed ever seen the light, it would have proved a work of deep interest. Affairs were now becoming serious. The side Ossoli had taken in politics precluded all hope of his ever recovering even a portion of his patrimony ; and there was small chance of his wife's book being published unless she returned to America.

The wedded pair were too poor to engage a passage in a steamer, so they procured accommodation on a merchant sailing vessel, which left Leghorn in May, 1850, with the expectation, which was fulfilled, of the voyage occupying two months. When in sight of land a hurricane arose, and the ship, heavily laden with marble, was wrecked, and nearly all lives were lost. The steward charged himself with the little Angelo, promising to save the child or lose his life in the attempt. He kept his word, for their bodies were washed on shore. But " Give back the dead, thou sea ! " is often a vain call, even when it is but the lifeless form for which we beg ; and the vast

Atlantic was the grave of Margaret and her husband.
The senseless Italian marble that had been intended
for the sculptor's chisel, broke a hole in the ship, and
dragged down the manuscript history of the siege of
Rome, to which I have already referred.

CHAPTER XIII.

A triad of single women—Mary Russell Mitford, Geraldine
Jewsbury, and Frances Brown the blind poetess.

MY. acquaintance with Mary Russell Mitford began
in rather a singular manner. It must have been in
1852 that a gentleman, whom we often saw, talked
more than ever of Miss Mitford, whom he had long
known, both personally and by a very voluminous
correspondence. He spoke of her always with the
affectionate admiration so becoming in one of a
younger generation who revered those whom he
looked on as leaders in the past. At this time Miss
Mitford was three or four years past sixty, and
resided in the cottage at Swallowfield, made famous
by her occupation of it. Physically, she was old and
infirm for her age, but her mental faculties seemed
but little impaired. She was engaged in the good
work of writing a book of recollections, with the
view of making some little provision thereby for her
two old servants. The mutual—I beg pardon,
common—friend to whom I have alluded must have
spoken to Miss Mitford of me with some kindliness,

for the authoress sent me gracious messages; and by-and-by it was intimated to me that she would be very happy to accept the dedication of a novelette of mine on the eve of publication. This intimation led to a correspondence, which grew more and more cordial; for Miss Mitford wrote charming letters in all but the great essential, legibility. Not only was her handwriting crabbed and imperfect, but she was parsimonious of paper, writing usually on half sheets, and habitually turning the envelopes of letters which she herself received, making them do duty a second time. I thought her kindness of heart must be extreme, for the dedication which I drew up and sent for her approval she declared was too cold and formal to be of service to "Lydia;" and she may be said to have prompted the more familiar one which appeared.

In my heart of hearts—but to my shame, I suppose —I had never greatly admired the village stories which had made Miss Mitford's reputation; but I had a keen recollection of the delight with which, in my girlhood, I had witnessed the representation of her tragedy of *Rienzi*. I am nearly sure it was that fine old actor, Charles Young, who took the part of the hero, and the Miss Phillips, to whom I have already alluded, who played the heroine. At any rate, it dwelt in my memory as a fine play magnificently acted. Bulwer Lytton referred to it in connection with his novel on the same subject; and it must have possessed considerable merit to have had a run on the London stage. I believe it was by this tragedy that my reverence for Mary Russell Mitford was mainly sustained. Certainly I was in a frame of mind to be gratified when she expressed a wish for me to pay her a few hours' visit before the summer was over.

Accordingly, a day was fixed; and one morning, in the month of August, I think, I started from Blackheath early enough to catch a train which left London Bridge at nine o'clock in the morning, my destination being a rural station, the name of which I forget, but which was the one nearest to Swallowfield. I had been told that on arriving at this station I should be sure to find some conveyance that would carry me to my destination; but at the end of my railway journey, I was rather dismayed to find that I had nine miles still to travel. Moreover, no public conveyance was attainable; I could procure only a tall gig, with the ostler, as I suppose he was, of a country inn for driver. I had long had a horror of two-wheeled vehicles, and mounted to my seat with fear and trembling. In something over an hour the distance was traversed, and we drew up at Miss Mitford's cottage door. It was by this time about one o'clock; and I arranged with the driver to remain in the village, in readiness to take me back about six o'clock, that I might meet the return train. I had a bad headache, which I was obliged to admit to my hostess; for I felt really ill from fatigue and excitement. But half an hour's rest, an ablution, and a little suitable refreshment might have brought me round. It is true I was offered some greasy sandwiches and a glass of very indifferent wine; but Miss Mitford, only lately risen and breakfasted— she was, indeed, coming down the stairs as I entered —was bent on taking me a drive through Strathsfield-saye Park, and had ordered her little pony carriage to be ready. She did not seem at all to realize that I was dazed and wearied; so I was hurried into the back seat of the four-wheeled chaise. Miss Mitford, of course, sitting, with a multitude of wraps, beside her man-servant, the driver.

I yield to no one in reverence for the great Duke of Wellington, and consequently could not fail to be interested in the stately home conferred on him by a grateful country; but physical suffering and mental enjoyment are not well mated. Miss Mitford leaned back sideways to talk to me, while I had to lean forward to listen and rejoin. That drive seemed even more miserable than the previous nine miles of jolting. But it came to an end, like pleasanter things, and her sympathetic woman-servant—wife, I believe, to the man-servant—conducted me to a room where I had the refreshment of soap and water. Then I went down to the little drawing-room, where my hostess was ready for conversation. She inti-mated to me that she "never dined," but that dinner would be ready for me by-and-by. Miss Mitford's habits were very eccentric, and not conducive to health and longevity. She habitually sat up till the small hours of the morning, and frequently till four or five o'clock. Of course she rose very late, and I understood that her breakfast between twelve and one o'clock was her principal meal of the day. Of medium height, but very stout, she moved with difficulty, and by the aid of a stick; but her large head and ponderous brow gave her a marked individuality. She had a pleasant voice, the trained voice of good breeding and of good society, with a certain touch of authoritativeness in it. Those who have been more in society, than feeble health has for many years permitted me to be, admit that really fine manners are a something that seems to grow rarer and rarer. But I can remember the fine manners of a past generation; and they were of two sorts, each revealing character very distinctly. There was the stately measured politeness, that was never ruffled by enthusiasm, never for a moment off guard; and there was the genial, kindly politeness—every whit as dignified as the other—but which, seeming to be of the nature born, has no need to be on guard.

I am obliged to confess that Miss Mitford's manners impressed me with the idea of being of the first-named sort. In the hour and a half which preceded my summons to a solitary dinner, we conversed on many subjects and spoke of many

people, and, it is a fact, that of not one celebrity did
she speak well, with the single exception of Louis
Napoleon, whose recent *coup d'état* she extenuated.
Robert Browning was the especial object of her
vituperation—little imagining that his career would
culminate in a grave in Westminster Abbey. She
thought he might as well have proposed to a princess
as to her friend, Elizabeth Barrett, whom she
evidently looked on as a naughty child for accepting him. Although not then so well acquainted
with the poet-pair, as I afterwards had the happiness
to become, I yet ranked them already as my friends,
and ventured, rather warmly, to defend them. I
doubt if she had read a line of Robert Browning's
later poems—and I doubt, also, if she had ever
pierced to the depths of those which his wife had
written. She had a personal liking for the poetical
girl-friend, who still looked up to her as a luminary ;
but in the Valhalla of souls I think the worship
needed to be reversed.

Reflecting on what she has done, and what her
opinions, as she expressed them in conversation,
seemed to be, my impression of Mary Russell Mitford
remains as that of a "hard-headed" woman, spoiled
by early and easily acquired literary success, at a time
when women authors were few ; whose intimate
friends seemed all in good positions, and who was
quite out of touch with the struggles of the middle-
classes. Yet I am sure she must have had tender

springs in her nature which circumstances had never called into play.

When the dreadful gig arrived to take me back to the station, I was still miserably ill, a fact which my hostess scarcely recognized, but we parted cordially, she giving me an engraving from the lifelike portrait of her by John Lucas, with an affectionate inscription in her own handwriting. I never saw Miss Mitford again. Soon after my visit her ·health failed more and more, and she died, mainly, I believe, from decay of nature, a year or two afterwards.

At the time that Miss Mitford spoke to me of the Brownings, they had been married some years; but the following letter, besides being of domestic interest, shows that the friendly relationship between the author of " Our Village " and " Rienzi " and the poetess still continued, in spite of the disfavour with which the elder lady had regarded the marriage.

> " 58, Welbeck Street, Cavendish Square,
> " Wednesday morning [Sept. 15th, 1852].

"MY DEAR MRS. CROSLAND,

"I reproach myself much in respect to you. I only hope, from your goodness, that you are more inclined to be indulgent to me than I am to myself.

"The *meaning* of my silence has not, however, been "the bad thing about it." I put off writing to you till I could have it in my power to fix a day for going to you, as you kindly proposed, and the press of our engagements not admitting of this, week after week I still waited, waited—and now my nurse has gone to visit her mother, and I have my child on my hands, with all the nursing, dressing, washing, and general state of imprisonment belonging to the privilege.

"Will you—can you forgive me? Do you understand how the chains are heavy upon my hands and feet?

"I have not been able to get down to Miss Mitford, though she has wished it and though I have wished it doubly.

"My nurse returns at the end of next week; but I can't answer for myself now, and had better say so. Is there no hope of seeing you here when you come to town? which may happen occasionally.

"I heard from our friend Mrs. Ogilvy* the other day, she seems quite well and happy, scheming vaguely about the Continent. By the way, a story of hers has been coming out of late in your periodical, which I have made some ineffectual efforts to get a sight of. Is it very improper of me if I ask you to lend me the numbers which contain it? If so, don't mind me. But if you have those numbers by you, and

---

* A lady better known by her initials E. A. H. O. than by her full name, and recognized as a writer of clever stories and able criticisms, as well as of spirited poems. Her volume entitled "A Book of Highland Minstrelsy," though differing in subjects treated, deserves to be compared for vigour and national enthusiasm with Professor Aytoun's "Lays of the Scottish Cavaliers."

can send them by the Parcel Delivery Company without inconvenience, I will return them to you carefully and thank you much besides.

"Oh, and I have to thank you twice over for 'Lydia,' now I have read the book. May all our talents in England have such pure aims!

"Most truly yours,

"ELIZABETH BARRETT BROWNING."

It would be difficult to imagine two "single women of a certain age" more different than were Miss Mitford, and Geraldine Endsor Jewsbury, though, for the matter of ages, the latter was a comparatively young woman when I first knew her. Small and slight, lithe and active, and with regular features, she must have been, what I always heard she was, a very pretty girl. Belonging to a Manchester family, I believe she came to London—though not then to reside in the metropolis permanently—about the time her elder sister married and went to India, where unhappily she soon died. This elder sister, some dozen years older than Geraldine, won fame as a poetess and as a writer of religious and moral essays and sketches; and I remember in my own girlhood how popular her works were. I think I paired off her poetry with that of the Rev. Thomas Dale, whose verses, like hers, were, in the early days of albums, often copied out to enrich them. But the literary productions of the two sisters were so different that it would be invidious to contrast or compare them.

Geraldine's talents were very varied, and she exercised them through long years in a most industrious manner. Her novels—especially "The Half Sisters" "Marian Withers" and "The Sorrows of Gentility"—showed that she possessed the resources necessary to form a great novelist. A quick, though quiet observer, a shrewd judge of character, with great command of language, shown often in epigrammatic wit, either in conversation or with the pen, she never failed to express her meaning lucidly. She was a very intimate friend of the Carlyles; and one writer speaks of her mind having been influenced by Carlyle's writing; but that was eminently the case with many men and women of her generation. From every great writer there emanates a wide-spreading influence, and as time passes on the dross of it falls away. Carlyle was not a demi-god; but, perhaps, the reason he is a little underrated now is that he did his work so well that many of the abuses he attacked have been swept away.

I think, however, that Geraldine Jewsbury was more especially the friend of Mrs. Carlyle than of her husband. I remember one occasion when I called on Miss Jewsbury, Mrs. Carlyle was announced as a visitor also; she was richly but soberly attired, and came in her carriage—what a contrast to those

early conditions of struggle and privation with which
the world is now acquainted! The visit occurred a
year or two before Mrs. Carlyle's sad death in Hyde
Park, when Geraldine Jewsbury was one of the two
friends who were summoned to St. George's Hospital
to identify the body. She spoke of the occasion to
me, but with great emotion. She told me also the story
of "the candles," some account of which has crept into
print, or I should refrain from repeating it, though
surely it does honour to both of the dead! Geraldine
knew that in the early days of her married life Mrs.
Carlyle had been rebuked on some occasion by her
mother for burning more candles than were necessary.
Not content with extinguishing them, she had put
them carefully away, keeping them, as a memento,
through the long years in a closet in her bedroom.
Not only had Geraldine the sad task of identifying
the body; she also looked on the remains of her
beloved friend, as she lay in her coffin just before
the lid was closed down; then the sudden thought
came to her that these treasured candles should be
buried with the dead. She knew where to find them,
and with her own hand placed them in the coffin.

Geraldine Jewsbury had many staunch friends, and
was herself a staunch friend to many. She was one
of the most sincere persons I ever knew. Her connection with the *Athenæum* was well known, and
she was often consulted on literary matters; but she
had so strong a sense of duty that I do not think

for her best friend she would have written a word of undeserved praise, or for her worst enemy—if she had enemies—a word of unmerited censure. Also, she read for publishers, an occupation that I cannot but think helped to impair her eyesight, which failed greatly at last. In reading the manuscripts submitted to her I know she always conscientiously considered her duty to her employers, knowing very well that many works might have merits that appealed only to the few, and could not be published under the same conditions as those likely to be instantly popular. She had very broad sympathies, but I am sure that no work, however clever, with the trail of the serpent about it would have received her "recommendation."

I think it is to be regretted that Geraldine Jewsbury did not give fuller scope to her powers of original writing ; but, after all, the world is indebted to her for much refined and subtle criticism, and, probably, for the publication in good time of many valuable works, that might have long lain dormant but for her insight and the judgment formed upon it. Of course these double duties must have established the mental attitude of looking critically on all books that came before her ; and, moreover, when literary plans and projects were discussed before her, or her opinion was asked, her advice was always most valuable. She had, too, the happiest manner of indicating a fault or a weak spot, always, while

pointing it out, recognizing the merit that made it
" such a pity " to leave the imperfection standing.   I
am certain it gave her real pleasure to praise, and
more or less pain to censure.

Allowing for the very different circumstances of
their lives, I think there were several points of similarity between Geraldine Jewsbury and Mrs. Carlyle,
of whom I had some knowledge before the occasion
to which I have referred.   Such points of similarity
are often to be observed among very intimate friends
—perhaps they are partly the occasion of the friendship, and are fostered by it.   Charles Dickens, who
did not much admire literary women, is reported to
have said that Mrs. Carlyle had more talent than the
" whole pack of them."   I think those were his words.
In my opinion Mrs. Carlyle was one of the cleverest
women in the world, and might have distinguished
herself in the same fields of literature as her friend,
had she so willed it.   But she was so true a woman
that all her ambition centred in, and was for her
husband.   Indeed the world is little likely to know
its indebtedness to her as the prop of the Chelsea
home, and the smoother of difficulties that stood in
the way of Carlyle's work.   Like Geraldine Jewsbury,
she was always loyal to her own sex.   Both talked
well in the old-fashioned style of good conversation-
alists—that is, without arguing or haranguing ; each
had a quick appreciation of circumstances, and the
happy faculty of seeing clearly what was morally

right to do, and also the expediency from a worldly
point of view, often by some happy suggestion, of
reconciling the two courses. Both were witty, even
satirical sometimes, but without malice. One of
Geraldine Jewsbury's most severe little speeches,
à propos of theological cant, was the wish that certain
people could be "poisoned with a decoction of their
own tongues." And once she said a wiser thing
when she declared that "no one was good for anything until well broken-up by suffering."

I am tempted to make this chapter a triad of
single-woman authoresses, as diverse in their genius
as they were in the circumstances of their lives. The
present generation seems to know nothing of Frances
Brown, the blind poetess; but about the middle of
the century her name was well before the world, and
a few years later her merits were sufficiently recognized for her to receive a government pension. I
cannot remember what incident it was that led to
our acquaintance, but well recollect her coming by
appointment to spend an afternoon with us. Of
course she was accompanied by the sister who had
so long been devoted to her, and whose subsequent
marriage doubtless made a great change in Frances
Brown's way of life. They were the daughters of
the village postmaster at Shanorlar, county Donegal;
and Frances lost her sight, at three years of age, from
virulent small-pox, as I heard. The family must have

R

been somewhat superior to their station for the blind girl to have profited, as we are told she did, by the lessons of her brothers and sisters. I found my visitors well-bred gentlewomen, whose fluent and interesting conversation was only rendered the more piquant by the slight Irish brogue which flavoured it. The first thing which struck me in Frances was her very exquisite figure, set off to advantage by a simple but well-fitting dress. She was just about, or but slightly above the middle height, and a painter or sculptor would have delighted in the lines of beauty that were revealed in her movements. I remember also thinking she would have been handsome but for the darkened vision, and some most disfiguring vestiges of the fell disease which had afflicted her. She moved with such ease that it was difficult at first—and until some little incident was evidence of it—to believe in her infirmity. Her memory was most retentive, and her mind singularly receptive, for she seemed fairly well acquainted with the topics of the day and its current publications, and, better still, with many sterling works which are the glory of English literature.

There is always something intensely pathetic in genius deprived of its needful culture; but God's ways are not man's ways, and there must be some hidden purpose in the cases of arrested mental development which we often see. When we consider the touching and graceful verses of Frances Brown—not to mention her prose works—we can but vaguely conjecture what she might have done under happier circumstances. It is truly said that the poet is "born, not made," and yet, of all mental workers, he surely requires wide, varied, and ever-increasing culture. If he has it not we can but expect from him the outpourings of his own emotions and experiences, instead of the broad sympathy and extended knowledge which enable him to revivify some dead hero, or present to our mind's eye great events, with life-like reality embalming them for ever—as our greatest poets have done—through the spell of poetic elucidation and imagery. The poetic gift is surely something like a fountain that requires to be perpetually fed by mountain streams. Alas for the poets, blind from infancy! alas for the peasant poets, from the typical one, Robert Burns, downwards, whose poetic faculty, if unbalanced by the highest moral nature, more often unfits them for the useful and active duties of life than renders them happy! But, fortunately for the world, there are "mute inglorious Miltons," who are not aspiring, but who, by patience and self-sacrifice, unconsciously make of their lives acted poetry. To them be the honour and reverence with which they but seldom meet!

CHAPTER XIV.

A serious chapter—Professor de Morgan—Rev. J. G. Wood—Sir
George Barker, K.C.B.—Robert Chambers—Professor Ansted—
Professor Skinner.

THE years from 1854 to 1857, inclusive, formed a
very memorable period to several eminent persons,
with whom I had the privilege of being acquainted.
I am very unwilling to offend deep-rooted prejudices,
which may originally have had "a leaning to virtue's
side," at the same time I should be a moral craven—
which I am happy to believe a woman seldom is—
if I omitted from the record of my recollections
circumstances which not a few persons have considered the most important in their lives.   I allude
to that outpouring of spiritual manifestations which
came upon the world about the period mentioned
above.

Let me begin by saying that I never, but once, paid
a shilling to a professional medium, and that once
was at the urgent solicitation of a friend, and when
visiting a seer.   Nor did I ever attend a public
seance.   My experience came through the medium-

ship of private friends, personages of unblemished character, and of intellect far above the average. First on the list I may mention a lady, now the widow of a physician, but whose name, as she happily still lives, I will refrain from mentioning. From royalty downwards she has been an influence in numerous lives, in breaking up the rusty fetters of materialism, or in making stable a wavering faith in immortality and in the unseen powers which surround us. Some of the communications received through her have been more explanatory of, or suggestive of, profound truths, than any theological or philosophical work I can call to mind.

Of established facts nothing can be more certain than that up to the time of the Reformation all Christendom not only believed in the reality of spiritual beings that were constantly about us, but that, under some circumstances, they manifested their presence; and, happily, the Anglican Prayer-book retains abundant evidence of such faith being only proper to the Christian mind. The great nations of antiquity had a like belief, which may be traced back through all history to its earliest records; and, though we over-elated nineteenth-century people, "heirs of all the ages," fancy ourselves lifted on to their shoulders, it may be that in our vain attempts to reach that eminence we sometimes slip down to be really at their feet. It was better to believe in Charon and the Elysian Fields than to be a rank materialist; and it is admitted that the fantasies of the heathen mythology contained suggestions of truth that were the preparation for the Divine light that was to come on the world.

All the creeds that throughout the long ages have sustained the human soul agree in one particular, that is, in the conflict between good and evil which is constantly going on about us. What is called modern spiritualism is full of warnings on this subject; and, from the experience of nearly half my long life, I would implore seekers for knowledge on this subject to be on their guard, and to remember that when the door which communicates with the outside world is opened—as it is by mediumship—foes as well as friends can enter. I speak reverently of the Bible when I remind my readers that it is throughout a history of spiritual manifestations, and of miracles— in other words, of higher laws superseding ordinary ones.

This universal belief is the primary fact which should make sceptics hesitate, with some approach to humility, and, rightly understood, must, to the believing student of history and biography, make what have been stumbling-blocks to thousands fall symmetrically into their places, like the pieces of a puzzle map, each a separate truth, yet harmonizing with all the rest.

Let me, however, proceed to the mention of names. About the year 1863 there was published by Messrs.

Longman and Co. a thick octavo volume, entitled,
" From Matter to Spirit;" though I do not
think the phrase "an open secret" was then adopted,
it would exactly have applied to the authorship of
this book. On the title-page is printed, "by C. D,"
and the preface is signed "A. B."; but it was widely
known that the body of the work was written by
Mrs. de Morgan, being the record of her ten years'
personal experience of spiritual phenomena, and
that the preface was written by her husband, the
grave and learned professor of mathematics and
writer on logic. I propose to extract the opening
paragraphs of this preface, the cautious wording of
which excites the admiration of a thoughtful reader,
so opposite is it to the unreasoning fervour of a
fanatic.

" It is but now and then that a preface is contributed by one who is
not the author ; and only now and not then, or then and not now, that
the writer of the preface declares he will not stand committed either *for*
or *against* the conclusions of the book. But this happens in the present
case. I am satisfied by the evidence of my own senses of *some* of the
facts narrated : of some others I have evidence as good as testimony can
give. I am perfectly convinced that I have both seen and heard in a
manner which should make unbelief impossible, things *called* spiritual
which cannot be taken by a rational being to be capable of explanation
by imposture, coincidence, or mistake. So far I feel the ground firm
under me. But when it comes to what is the cause of these phenomena,
I find I cannot adopt any explanation which has yet been suggested.
If I were bound to choose among things which I can conceive, I should
say *there is some combination of will, intellect, and physical power, which
is not that of any of the human beings present.* But thinking it very
likely that the universe may contain a few agencies, say half a million,
about which no man knows anything, I cannot but suspect that a small

proportion of these agencies—say five thousand—may be severally competent to the production of all the phenomena, or may be quite up to the task among them. The physical explanations I have seen are easy, but miserably insufficient ; the spiritual hypothesis is sufficient but ponderously difficult. Time and thought will decide, *the second asking the first for more results of trial.*"

The last italics are mine, adopted to mark a most significant sentence. The professor's preface extends to upwards of forty pages of learned and philosophic writing, but, instead of the spiritual theory being weakened, every other hypothesis seems eliminated, though without exact avowal of the fact. Mrs. de Morgan was a remarkably clear-headed, conscientious woman, and relates, for the most part, experiences that occurred under her own roof, with mediums who were members of her family or household.

The next authority I shall cite is the Rev. J. G. Wood, the well-known naturalist. He might well be a believer in spiritual communications, for he was himself a medium for them. About the year 1857 he had occasion to write to me on the subject, and about some original translations he was making— from St. Paul's Epistles, I think they were—which he considered harmonized with our experiences, and he added in a parenthesis, "the raps have been going on all the time while I was writing the translation." He was, to some extent, a seeing medium as well as a rapping one, occasionally discerning the atmosphere about people. But, an enlightened Biblical student, and strong in his faith, he was one of those who might be said not to need spiritualism ; and, having once or twice been deceived by " lying spirits " in his later years, I believe he rather resisted the influence than encouraged it. He was fully convinced of the apparitions of animals, as well as of human beings, and in his very interesting work, " Man and Beast," he boldly argues, and on Biblical authority, in favour of the immortality of all creatures which have breathed the breath of life.

Next I will cite the honoured name of Brigadier-General Sir George Barker, K.C.B.,* only Colonel Barker, C.B., when we first knew him, shortly after his return from the Crimea, where he had greatly distinguished himself. Now, I think it will be conceded that an artillery officer must, from the nature of his studies and duties, be a man of some strength of mind, a mathematician of no mean order, and one well qualified to reason on cause and effect. Such a man, undoubtedly, was Sir George Barker, somewhat reticent in manner, as deep thinkers often are, though keenly observant. Yet he was not only a believer in the spiritual manifestations he witnessed, but a writing medium himself. Though ordered to India immediately on the news of the mutiny reaching England, he found half an hour out of the brief time at his disposal to do us the honour of calling to say farewell,

---

* His widow, as Lady Barker, won for herself an honourable literary position, until by her second marriage she merged the name into that of Lady Broome.

in recognition of, what he was pleased to consider, spiritual privileges under our roof.

In mentioning the names of eminent persons with whom I was personally acquainted, who, after careful investigation, were steadfast believers in the truth of spiritual phenomena, I must not omit my dear friends Mr. and Mrs. S. C. Hall, and also William and Mary Howitt, and their daughter Anna Mary, afterwards Mrs. Watts. As, however, they have all left behind them their testimony on the subject, I need not enlarge on it. Yet I may mention that Anna Mary was a very powerful medium, the mediumship showing itself in various ways. I have myself seen her hand seized and guided, apparently more against her will than in accordance with it ; and drawings, generally of a symbolic character, were produced under the influence, without her knowing what they meant, until interpreted by some other method of communication.

I well remember, on one special occasion, this sort of thing occurring, when her hand had a pencil in it, and she seemed forced to draw on a scrap of paper, that chanced to be on the table, though wholly unconscious of what she was going to produce. The drawing proved to be a very elaborate one, yet did not occupy more than a very few minutes. But I mention the circumstance because, during the process, which I watched with interest, I distinctly saw a minute spark of light at the point of the pencil, which was a common cedar one.

Of course, as Miss Howitt, in her normal state, was a very charming artist, sceptics doubted the inspiration which produced these symbolic drawings ; but, besides that, she was a woman of a most sensitive conscience, and no one could witness such a little incident as I have described and retain any doubt on the subject. Indeed, I consider she was one of the martyrs to the cause of truth, for the different manifestations which came through her exhausted her physical frame ; and, of all the similarly endowed people I have known, she seemed the least capable of resisting the influence when it came upon her. That there is a resisting and an encouraging of the power there can be no doubt.

I now come to a name that is worthy of being bracketed with the noblest of those I have mentioned. I allude to that of my old and valued friend Robert Chambers, of whom mention is made in an earlier chapter. Always a lover and seeker of truth, he was one of the earliest investigators of the phenomena of which I am writing. Too patient and careful to be quick in forming a decided opinion, years of investigation passed before he arrived at a definite conclusion. He had, in a quiet manner, weighed all arguments on the phenomena ; but, like Professor de Morgan, was convinced that imposture or co-

incidence could not account for them.   Every one
will admit that a conjuror may produce a clumsy
imitation of such things, but then he must be provided with, at least, a barrow-load of apparatus.
I say a "clumsy" imitation, because no one accustomed to the genuine raps has ever confounded
imitations with them ; and the liftings, the tiltings,
and the removal of heavy articles to a distance,
accomplished by the would be "exposers," all require
mundane appliances.   But our friend, the young lady
medium, through whom such wonderful things happened, brought no machinery with her.   A fan and
pocket-handkerchief, and, perhaps, a scent-bottle, were
the most I ever saw her carry, and I doubt if her light
summer dresses had even pockets in them.   I think
when Robert Chambers, Sir George Barker, and Mr.
Wood met at our house, it was a great satisfaction to
find themselves in accord, and about equally interested
in the young lady to whom they were owing so much.
On one occasion, when we had a little gathering of
like-minded investigators, the room in which we sat
was shaken as by a storm, yet in a manner impossible
fully to describe.   The floor vibrated under our feet,
and the window-shutters rattled, as if they would
burst from their fastenings, and for a few seconds I
feared the house was in danger.   I believe we all felt,
but reverently I hope, that it recalled that passage in
the second chapter of the Acts of the Apostles in
which it is said, "And suddenly there came a sound

from heaven as of a rushing mighty wind, and it filled
all the house where they were sitting."

I remember Robert Chambers was greatly struck
by this occurrence, and realized what an aid to belief
in miracles some experience of the phenomena was.
He was among the first who perceived that, while the
laws which regulate "matter" are undoubtedly rigid
and inflexible, the laws which regulate "spirit" are
hidden from us on the other side of the veil.
Electricity, magnetism, and, probably, other but unknown imponderable forces form the bridge between
the two. I believe it was Mrs. Browning who first
applied the phrase *tertium quid* to these forces.

Robert Chambers was a great friend of D. D.
Home's, and it was said that he was the "literary
friend" who wrote the introductory remarks to Mr.
Home's book, entitled "Incidents in my Life;" and
I see no reason to doubt it. I believe he had the
same opinion of Mr. Home as that which was held
by the butler of some friends of ours, at whose
house Mr. Home used to stay, sometimes for weeks
together. When the great medium was exposed to
cruel slander, some of which, of course, reached the
servants' hall, one of the ladies of the family spoke
to the butler on the subject, the man replying,
"Lor', miss, Mr. Home's too simple a creature to
deceive even a child."

I only saw Mr. Home three times, but thought
there was something very unaffected and winning

about him ; and I knew several of his most intimate friends, who all spoke of him with respect and
affection.   Robert Chambers and Mr. and Mrs. S. C.
Hall were among those who esteemed him most
highly.

I think Robert Chambers was the first to notice
that the movement of our table always began by
adjusting itself due north and south.   As it stood in
the middle of the room it required the irregularity
of about six inches to render it so.   We had often
observed that the first token of the unseen intelligence was to make this movement ; and one evening
Robert Chambers took a little compass from his pocket,
it having occurred to him that, where magnetism
was so distinctly associated with the phenomena, it
would be desirable to verify precisely the aspect of
the house.   From the beginning he investigated with
patience and acumen.   The letters he wrote to me
on the subject were headed "private," and, of course,
treated as such ; but, though for a long time reticent
to the world at large on the subject of spiritualism,
that he could speak of it among friends the following
extract from a letter I received from Mrs. Crowe will
show.   The letter is dated 3, Porchester Terrace
(Mrs. Loudon's residence), Friday, May 15th—there
ought have been added, 1857.

"I came to town last Wednesday, and this morning
Robert Chambers has called and told us of the
wonders that are doing at Blackheath.   I had heard

something of the sort from Mr. John Barker * and
was intending to write to you and ask for the
Loudons and myself the favour of an interview with
Miss A., but R. C. tells me you are going from home
and cannot receive any more. Under the circumstances, can any other arrangement be made? or will
it be better to wait till you return?"

The opinion of Robert Chambers on the manifestations, however, became at last pretty generally
known, and for many years past "Robert Chambers,
LL.D." has regularly appeared in the lists of eminent
adherents in the numerous publications devoted to
the subject. I ought to mention that, returning to
town after an evening at our house, he told a fellow
guest, likewise a literary man, that he had destroyed
a manuscript representing the labours of three years,
in consequence of the overthrow of old opinions
occasioned by the manifestations. I wonder if it was
some work on the same lines as the famous "Vestiges," a book allowed to remain "out of print" so
long before its author's death.

My "serious chapter" is nearly ended; but there
are still two circumstances I should like to mention.
Some time after the publication in one of Charles
Dickens's periodicals—*All the Year Round,* I think—of
that remarkable article, called "Mr. H.'s Narrative,"
I was invited to meet the artist at dinner by common

* Brother of Sir George.

friends for the express purpose of hearing the narra-
tion of his extraordinary adventure from his own lips.
I sat next him at dinner, and had as much conversation as it was easy to maintain with a man so deaf
that he used a trumpet. To be sure my object was
to listen, not to talk, and I had the satisfaction of
hearing Mr. Heaphy himself give the true, unvarnished
story, as he afterwards contributed it to *All the
Year Round* (No. 128, October 5th, 1861). The first
version which appeared was inaccurate in several
particulars, having been compiled from rumour, and
dressed up like an ordinary magazine article.

It is well worth reading as a singularly graphic
and interesting narrative of the spirit of a young
girl, whom in life he had never seen, appearing to
Mr. Heaphy to assist him in painting a portrait of
her, which the bereaved father had commissioned
him to execute from description and an imperfect
print of some one else, supposed to be like her.

In the summer of 1863 I spent a delightful ten
days with my dear old friends, Professor Ansted and
his accomplished wife. They then occupied Im-
pington Hall, a fine old-fashioned mansion, about
three miles from Cambridge. An excellent amateur
actor, a keen judge and admirable reader of poetry,
he was more many-sided than men of science usually
are. From the nature of his pursuits he had travelled
much, and mixed in the intellectual circles of nearly

every capital in Europe—by the way, I remember him
saying that the Athenian women were, as a rule, the
most cultivated of any he had found. But he took
only a languid interest in occult matters, though he
listened with respect to the accounts he heard from
many quarters of spiritual phenomena. Perhaps,
however, his comparative indifference was to be
accounted for by his thoroughness ; so that, had he
allowed himself deliberately to begin an investigation
of them, he would have found himself drawn away,
to an inconvenient degree, from those pursuits on
which he was imperatively engaged.

Being himself a Cambridge man, of course he had
the opportunity of showing to a visitor everything in
the University that was most interesting. Being
also an M.A., he knew, I suppose, all the dons ; and
among them I was introduced to a very interesting
old man of upwards of seventy years of age, Mr.
George Skinner, Professor of Hebrew. One evening
he spent at the Ansteds, and another we passed at
his house, mainly for the purpose of our conversing
on the subject of the spiritual phenomena, which, of
late years, had occupied so many thoughtful minds,
and of which a member of his family had been
the subject of some startling experience. He must
have been a man accustomed to weigh evidence,
for he listened attentively to all I said. His interest
warmed with my confirmation of much that he had
heard from another, and I remember that the tears

S

dimmed his eyes when he said, " How can I doubt, when M——, who never told me a lie, describes these things, and you say just the same ?   You cannot tell how happy it makes me to have the truth proved of what I have been teaching all my life ! "

Surely there are millions—yes, millions of people who, with a slight alteration, can echo these words and say, " How happy it makes us to have the truth proved of what the Bible has taught us all our lives ! "

CHAPTER XV.

Robert and Elizabeth Barrett Browning in Florence—Mr. Seymour
Kirkup—The sculptors, Hiram Powers, Gibson, and Paul Akers.

IN the autumn of 1857 I made arrangements with
friends to go abroad, and pass with them the winter
in Italy ; and I look upon the opportunity I had
of improving my acquaintance with Robert and
Elizabeth Barrett Browning as one of the most noteworthy circumstances of my month's sojourn in
Florence. Two or three kind notes, mostly on literary
matters, and a morning visit or two made up all the
personal acquaintance I could hitherto claim with her,
whom I revered as the greatest of poetesses, and yet
whom I seemed to know intimately from my deep
womanly sympathy with her revealings. The last is
not a haphazard word, for I hold that she does reveal
some heights and depths of woman's nature, in a
manner only to be rivalled in a very few instances by
the very few greatest poets.

Most kindly was I received by both husband and
wife in that Casa Guidi, which has been made famous
for ever, not only from having given a title to the

thrilling poem which tells of Italy's wrongs and aspirations, but from having been for many years the residence of its beloved author.   To see Italy a united kingdom, with rank and *prestige* among European powers, seems to me a thing over which we may well sing a *Te Deum*, and, oh, how Mrs. Browning would have rejoiced had she lived to witness it !   But instead of speculating on her feelings, let me describe her as best I can.

As, I think, in all palatial houses, the suite of rooms opened one into another.   Robert Browning himself ushered me, on my first visit, through one or two apartments to the drawing-room ; and in a minute or two the hostess entered by a door on the opposite side.   Certainly she was a little below the middle height, and the loftiness and spaciousness of the room served to make the fact more apparent, as she approached me with that gliding movement, which I think has gone out of fashion, but which in my early days used to be called swan-like.   There is a portrait of her, engraved from a photograph taken in 1859, that is an excellent likeness.   Her abundant hair, falling in long thick ringlets, was of chestnut brown, and her eyes were of a similar hue, with a softness and sweetness of expression not possible to describe. This first visit was very pleasant to me, but hardly so pleasant as subsequent ones, when we had become more intimate.   A *tête-à-tête* with Mrs. Browning was most enjoyable, for her conversation was delightful. Full of information of many sorts, when she agreed with what was said, she tossed back the thought which had pleased her, enlarged and embellished ; if she differed it was with a gentle regret, quite devoid of obstinate self-sufficiency. In truth, in every word and gesture she showed the good breeding which, grafted on such a nature, had rendered her manners perfectly charming.

We spent an evening at Casa Guidi. I say "we," because my friends were kindly invited with me ; and one of them, a lover of light, said, in jest, long afterwards, that though she had called twice on Mrs. Browning, and passed an evening at her house, she had never seen her. This was an allusion to the shade in which she delighted. By day anything like glare was excluded, and, besides, we always sat far from the windows ; in the evening the lamps were shaded—a delightful arrangement, according to my feelings. Very curious is it to note the manner in which light affects different persons. We read of Dickens writing in a room flooded with sunshine, while many persons there are who cannot even think clearly in any sort of strong light. I believe there is many a schoolgirl, and, perhaps, sensitive schoolboy, who is held back in the educational race by being subjected to the strong light, which some scientists have written about as being good for everybody.

On the evening we spent at Casa Guidi, Mrs.

Browning presided at the tea-table, and the hissing urn was a pleasant reminder of England. T. A. Trollope was of the little party, a man not so widely known as his brother, for his genius was of the rare sort that appeals to the few rather than to the many. As much at heart a Florentine as I think the Brownings were, his stories of Italian life are unique in their excellence. He wrote also with great force on the state of Italian affairs. Public events of course became a theme of conversation. The Indian mutiny was only just quelled; British troops had been conveyed to the scene of action through France, and the *entente cordiale* between England and France was a source of rejoicing to most people. Very naturally, the conversation glided into a discussion on Louis Napoleon— of his antecedents, his character, and his present position as emperor. I found it a rare treat to listen —if I may use a metaphor—to the clash of weapons in the wordy battle which followed, Mrs. Browning upholding her opinion of his wisdom, his genius, and general nobility of character against weighty arguments brought forward by her husband and Mr. Trollope. The late Lord Lytton, then Mr. Lytton, was to have been their guest that evening, but was not well enough to venture out on a wet night, and sent an apology for his absence. I wonder which side the future ambassador, already in diplomatic training, would have taken.

I think no one, remembering Mrs. Browning's long and fervid, but certainly one-sided poem, " Crowned and Buried," could wonder that some of her enthusiasm for the first emperor had survived to be bestowed on the nephew ; and her warmth brought back to my mind the talk to which I had listened in my childhood, when " Bonapartists " were discoursing on a subject of which they seemed never to weary. Could it be possible that she had some vague pre-vision of what Louis Napoleon would do for her beloved Italy, and what he would *be* for it in fact, inasmuch as his downfall was the occasion of the withdrawal of the French troops from Rome.

It was understood that Mrs. Browning, even in Florence, never went out between October and April, but one day her husband called on me with a special object. The last time I had seen the Brownings in England the conversation turned to the subject of the then recent spiritual manifestations which had been the talk of the town. Mrs. Browning was deeply interested in many things I had to tell her, her husband joining at first but little in the conversation between us. When, however, I offered to lend her a certain book on the subject, which she wished to see, he broke in, somewhat vehemently, begging I would do nothing of the kind, as he did not wish her mind to dwell on such things. I remember Mrs. Browning exclaiming rather warmly, " Robert, my soul is my own," though, with wife-like obedience, she yielded. But in Florence, with a smile on his face, Robert Browning asked me if I chanced to have that book with me, as now he had no objection to his wife reading it! I did chance to have it with me, and promptly fetched it from an adjoining room, and in two minutes, without being at all examined, it was slipped into the borrower's deep coat-pocket.

I have always been puzzled at Robert Browning's subsequent violent antagonism to what is called " spiritualism," for at the time I mention he appeared to have quite got over his first repugnance to it, and must have respected a great many people who had wide experience of the phenomena. Of course the next time I called on Mrs. Browning the subject was freely discussed ; but, though deeply interested, she was perfectly calm and judicial, rejoicing, however, like the old professor of Hebrew, at every outward proof of the truth of her inward convictions. But there were many other things to talk about, and she liked well enough to speak of Florence and her darling son, then so delicate-looking a boy of eight or nine years old, that it gladdened as well as surprised me to hear of him about a dozen years later as one of the "Oxford Eight." He was a very precocious child. At the age I mention he was an accomplished linguist, and I saw him reading for amusement some French or German book, and Tuscan born and bred, Italian or English might equally be considered his mother tongue. Mrs.

Browning told me of an amusing incident in reference
to her son's critical ear for language. One day she
was speaking Italian in his presence, and had occasion
to use the small word " no," which it would appear is
a crucial test with foreigners. " Mamma dear," exclaimed the boy, " you'll never speak Italian as long·
as you live ! " repeating the word for her edification
with its true racy pronunciation. A few nights afterwards I heard the " no " spoken on the stage, and
thoroughly realized the difficulty it presented to an
English tongue. The boy was not only a linguist,
but thoroughly intelligent in many ways, and I heard
him play a duet with his father on the piano in a
charming manner.

On none of my pleasant visits to the Casa Guidi
had I the heart to comment on the absence of
" Flush "—whose acquaintance I had the honour of
making in London some years previously—knowing
well the mysterious depth and pathos there is in
dog love. I do not envy any one who can read,
without some tender memory or sympathetic emotion,
Mrs. Browning's touching poem to her dog Flush,
her " loving fellow-creature."

After the sojourn of a few weeks in Florence, the
day of leave-taking came. I will only say I kept
sacred the spot on my cheek, where her " woman's
kiss " rested, as long as I could, and carried away
with me the impression that closer knowledge of
Elizabeth Barrett Browning had made me revere and

love her more and more, had made me more and
more conscious that—

> " Never—never Woman's feet
> Clomb before to her high seat,
> Yet to her it seemeth meet;

> " For—true Woman stoopeth she
> To her sisters pityingly
> Teaching them beseechingly.

> " Telling truths ne'er heard before
> Opening wide the secret door
> Which they pressed against of yore,

> " Faintly, vaguely, murmuring low,
> ' Oh, for one to come and show
> All the Woman's soul must know.'"

The Florentines loved her well, and, in a few years,
all Italy, freed, must have joined in the tribute paid
by the people who knew her best. Over the entrance
to Casa Guidi is placed the following inscription,
written by Niccolo Tommaseo—

> " Qui scrisse e mori
> ELISABETTA BARRETT BROWNING,
> che in cuore di donna conciliava
> scienza di dotto e spirito di poeta,
> e fece del suo verso aureo anello
> fra Italia e Inghilterra
> Pone questa lapide
> Firenze grata.
> 1861."

" Here wrote and died Elizabeth Barrett Browning, who with her
woman's heart combined the soundest learning and a poet's genius, and
made by her verse a golden link between Italy and England.   Grateful
Florence places this memorial stone.   1861." *

---

* It is almost presumptuous to attempt a translation of this very

Shortly before I left Florence, Robert Browning took me to call on Mr. Seymour Kirkup, that interesting old bachelor, who, already somewhat of a celebrity, became more famous a few years later in consequence of his discovery of Giotto's portrait of Dante. I wish I could describe him as I think he deserves to be described, but I only saw him once. He was an English *savant*, but I understood had not visited England for more than thirty years. I suppose few men could have said more conscientiously than he could, "My mind to me a kingdom is." From all I heard and the little I saw of him I should judge that he lived mainly in the inner world of thought. Evidently a man of independent means, he seemed quite regardless of appearances. He occupied a house at the southern end of the Ponte Vecchio, his windows looking out on the Arno. We were ushered into a lofty, spacious apartment, which struck me instantly—and the impression has remained unchanged—as the very type of a mediæval laboratory ; and when Mr. Kirkup entered the room, attired in a long flowing garment, presumably a dressing-gown, he seemed indeed the fit presiding deity.

The apartment was littered from end to end, and dust lay thick everywhere, showing itself of course most on polished surfaces, notably on an old square

idiomatic and expressive Italian—may some other hand have done it better.

piano, which was open, with music on and about it, and on the floor. There was no token of a servant's duster or woman's tidying having been there for ages. Globes may be in any gentleman's library without looking remarkable, but I think there must have been something hanging up or indicative of the astrologer's art, for me to have formed the rapid judgment which I did. That he drew horoscopes I heard long afterwards. But the excuse for my introduction to him was the little book about which there had been such a fuss, or perhaps I should say the subject of it, for Mr. Kirkup had had personal experiences of what is called spiritualism. He evidently had something very like contempt for the doubters; but I fear that the isolated old man, notwithstanding his learning and philosophy, had got hold of many things by the wrong end, and that his was perilously near, what in the Middle Ages was called, black magic. The spiritualism which has converted Agnostics into humble Christians, is not necromancy, but something far purer.

The visit was not a very long one, for, unless my memory cheats me, Mr. Kirkup was deaf, and Robert Browning sat listening to our conversation without taking part in it—an uncomfortable state of things for me, for much as I admired his genius and liked him for his many fine qualities, I was always a little afraid of Robert Browning; he could be so sarcastic. Yet, unless there was a grave fault that deserved chastising, I am sure that he never meant to wound, and when he had done so inadvertently I am equally certain that he would have been ready the next minute to perform a substantial service to the one he had hurt.

Mr. Kirkup lived to extreme old age—ninety or thereabouts—dying in 1880, I think. My slight acquaintance with him led to my knowing his sister, an infirm and nearly blind old woman, who proved to be a neighbour of ours at Blackheath. I often speculated on the strange life her brother had led for so many years, while she was pining to see him once more. "Judge not" is a solemn command, but it did seem sad that these two unwedded, close relations should be parted for half their lives by seas and mountains, and I cannot help thinking the brother would have been a happier man if he had cultivated a little more the affections of the heart, to balance the otherwise absorbing exercise of his mental powers—faculties that seemed mainly brought into play for his own solace and enjoyment. A little self-sacrifice often brings about a rich reward.

I have one or two other memories of Florence that seem to me worth recording. I took a letter of introduction from an American friend to Hiram Powers, known chiefly in England, I believe, as the sculptor of "The Greek Slave," a statue which attracted much attention in the Great Exhibition of

1851. I found him a very unaffected and interesting man, in the prime of life. Unfortunately, he had illness in his family, so that I did not see any of them; but his studio, like so many in Italy, was situated in a garden some distance from his house, and with no more disturbing noise about it than the rustle of the trees, not yet bare of their leaves, though it was the middle of October. The "Greek Slave" was there, of course, though probably not the identical one which had appeared in London, and I was at first a little amused by his depreciation of her. But when I looked round I began to understand his jealousy, for that word, I think, expresses to what his feeling amounted. Without detracting one iota from the merits of the "Slave," it must be admitted that the wan face and somewhat attenuated figure—so appropriate to the subject—did not always contrast favourably with the more serene, or more joyous expression of other works. I seem to recollect an Eve of surpassing beauty. A sculptor's fame ought to be one of the most lasting, and I hope that on the other side of the Atlantic, at any rate, Hiram Powers is recognized as one of America's greatest artists.

It must be remembered that in 1857 Italy was still in bondage, though, since the Crimean war especially, the eyes of patriots were turned hopefully northward to the little kingdom of Sardinia and its gallant king. One Sunday morning, as I was going to the Protestant

church, I saw chalked on a low wall opposite our hotel
the words, "Viva Victor Rè d'Italia." Of course I
found them obliterated when I came back, but they
were a sign of the smouldering fire, of which I had
other means of becoming perfectly aware. It was surprising the freedom with which on two or three occasions shopkeepers spoke of the political situation, and
of their hatred of the existing state of things, though I
really believe it was only to the English or American
they would so have spoken. Then there was an
Italian teacher, a scholarly man, recommended by the
Brownings, from whom I had a dozen lessons, who
enlightened me very much as to the discontent of the
people, and the tyranny under which they lived. It
appeared that the police had a right to enter a house,
and search for what they called seditious books or
papers; but Signor A—— chuckled over the fact that,
as he had an English wife, it was only necessary to
have her name written on anything for it to be safe.
It warms one's heart to feel that England's mantle is
broad enough to shelter her children all over the
world, and, even as in this case, to protect a foreigner
sometimes under its folds.

I am tempted to mention another little incident
which was gratifying to my feelings. We were
travelling by *diligence*, and found ourselves, about
midnight, at a barrier where passports had to be
examined. I think it was between the Tuscan and
Papal States. The vehicle drew up under a stone arch-

way, where ponderous gates had to be opened before we could proceed. I had charge of the document, which described the height, noses, eyes, etc., of all our little party, and, suddenly aroused from a dozing condition, I was rather slow in diving into a deep pocket for the passport. Meanwhile the hand of a young man of perhaps nineteen or twenty was eagerly stretched out, but before I had actually placed what he wanted in it, an older man appeared at the window, and exclaiming to his subordinate, " Inglese ! " waved back the passport. I think I never heard so much expressed by the intonation of a single word in my life. It meant, "You fool! cannot you see they are English! Don't bother them."

Another little personal anecdote I will venture on giving, solely for its comicality. One of my small troubles during that Italian tour was the impossibility of procuring so simple a thing as a plain biscuit, with which to supplement some unsatisfactory meal, or assuage the cravings of luncheon-time hunger; sweet cakes and dainty confections were to be had in abundance, but these were not what I wanted. I mentioned my distress in one of my letters to my husband, and he found means of sending me a case of Lemann's biscuits to Leghorn, where at a certain date we should arrive. Lemann was the one great biscuit provider of my youth, and with whom for many long years none seemed daring enough to compete. My treasure, a goodly case of about fifteen inches square, was a great temptation, but, as it was so much easier to carry about in its properly packed state than if disturbed, I determined not to open it until we were settled somewhere for at least a few days, and this did not happen until we reached Milan. I think the passport difficulty I am about to describe happened at Novara. The case of biscuits excited great curiosity among the custom-house officers. In vain I tried to explain that it contained "biscuits," "per mia salute." I had not the Italian "biscotto" at my tongue's end, but French was supposed to be understood. The chisel was just being inserted to lift the lid, when again an older official interfered, and, holding his fat, protecting hand like a dome over the case, stayed the opening, exclaiming to the other with a smile, "Bif steak—bif steak!" Again I attempted to set him right, but he only shook his head, with a compassionate expression, that seemed to say, "Why do you deny it?" Perhaps he has often told the story of the English ladies who were travelling with a case of "Bif steaks," if so, I hope his listeners have been as much amused as I am to this day when I recall the scene.

In Rome I became acquainted with the English sculptor, Gibson. He had recently completed his coloured Venus, of which he spoke with Pygmalion-like admiration. She had lately cost him two guineas,

T

he said, the price of a pair of gold earrings, which he pointed out dangling from her marble ears. Yet dangling is scarcely the word to use, for it implies something of movement ; and the charm of the earring lies, I think, in its perpetual motion. It may be only a silly fancy, but I confess to believing that the earrings helped to vulgarize the statue, making it still more realistic and less ideal than it already was. But, then, I did not like the coloured Venus which figured five years later in the London Exhibition of 1862.

Gibson was a worshipper of Greek art, the style and manner of which he copied successfully, though, in my humble opinion, with always something wanting which the ancients had. He said he believed in Jupiter. Yes, doubtless as a great pagan and poetical idea, but that was all. Of course there were some beautiful works in his studio ; but, somehow, there was a roughness about the man which made me less interested in him than I generally am in artists of all denominations.

Not far off was a studio where worked a young American sculptor, Paul Akers, whose productions were unquestionably of a high order. I think he could not have been thirty at the time of his death, which occurred two or three years after I first knew him ; therefore, I suppose, his works were looked on by friends and critics as rich in promise for the future as in performance. He was in delicate health when

I was in Rome, and said to be consumptive, but his energies seemed unflagging, and he was full of kindliness to a stranger in pointing out the beauties of ancient art, leaving her in a great measure to discover the merits of his own works. I have often wondered how far his brief career has been recognized in America. I only hope that he lived to see safely established in the "resurrection" of marble, two works which I saw in the "life stage" of the clay, for they certainly deserved immortality. One was a figure, about two feet high, of Saint Elizabeth of Hungary, at the moment when, at her husband's bidding, she opens her apron, and finds that the bread which—contrary to the tyrant's injunctions—she was carrying to the poor had been changed into roses. The glad surprise on the beautiful face—quite different from the wild wonder of one unacquainted with miracles—told the whole story with exquisite pathos. What a pair they must have been—the mediæval potentate and his saintly but slightly disobedient wife!

The other clay to which I allude was the recumbent figure of a drowned fisher-boy—pearl-fisher, I think—with the tangle of sea-weed about him to tell the story. It was a privilege to see these things in the manner I did, and I have often thought what a disadvantage it is for people to know great works only in the "death" state of the plaster, according to Thorwaldsen's definition of the three stages.

One more recollection of Rome, and it shall be the last. I saw the Pope, Pio IX., in St. Peter's on Christmas Day, 1857, as he was carried aloft in the state becoming the day. His appearance was that of a portly, good-tempered, good-natured old man, with a complexion as white as his pearly garments. I had long known that that blanched skin in the old was a token of length of days—it was remarkable in the first Duke of Wellington ; and I have noticed it in many cases.

CHAPTER XVI.

R. H. Horne—J. A. Heraud—Westland Marston.

I RETURNED to England in April, 1858, rich in memories, which are still a delight to me, and for some years I enjoyed the friendship, and, more or less, the society of many of the gifted ones whom I have mentioned in these pages. But failing health and waning sight, together with residing just far enough from London to render a little journey thither a toil and fatigue, made me drop away from the opportunities I might have had of bringing my recollections to a later date. But later recollections, which could only refer to what thousands living are able to chronicle, seem to me of less value than records of the decades which preceded the birth of the men and women who are now coming forward to move the world. The Great Reaper has been busy, for it may have been noticed that, except incidentally, I have refrained from writing about the living. Yet there are three authors I have yet to mention—dead within these few years—whom, for some reasons, it seems convenient to group together.

They are R. H. Horne, J. A. Heraud, and Dr. Westland Marston. Fifty years ago their names were familiar ones to the reading public of England, but they seem little mentioned now.

On the strength of his "Orion," I venture to rank Richard Hengist Horne as a true and fine poet, worthy to be ranked as such through all time. It has been said that the poet always represents his age; this is true to some extent, yet if he only shadows forth his age, the probability is that he will die with it. But there are eternal verities which do not belong exclusively to any period of time, and these are what R. H. Horne elucidates in his grand epic. "Orion" would have been as true a thousand years ago, and will be as true a thousand years hence as it is to-day.

It must have been about 1840 that the poem was published, and in the eccentric form, which probably is only remembered by elderly readers. For years it was spoken of as the "farthing epic," because originally it was published at that price, with a stipulation, however, that a purchaser was only to take one copy.

In the preface to a later, seven-shilling edition of the work, the author explains his motive. To use his own words would necessitate a very long quotation, but what he means and distinctly expresses is that, while he wished "Orion" to be known to the critics and lovers of poetry, he could not afford to publish it in the usual manner, sending copies to the press, to friends, and to many strangers. He was aware that the taste of the public was being so corrupted by the burlesque and caricature style of literature, which was then coming into vogue, that there was no chance of a new poem of so different an order paying its expenses. He thought, however, that curiosity might be piqued by the poem being offered for the smallest coin of the realm. The result was so far satisfactory that people did obtain the closely printed pages, and notwithstanding the fact that it is a grave disadvantage to a new poem to read it in small print and crowded lines, the work attracted attention and admiration, and became for awhile the town talk.

It must have been early in 1841 that I once met R. H. Horne. I was destined not to see him again for five or six and thirty years. He was at that time in the prime of life, and enjoying such fame as "Orion" had brought him. There had been a gathering of a party of literary people, who called themselves "syncretics," to which my mother and I had been invited. The syncretic society included several authors who had attained, or subsequently did attain fame, and among these certainly were R. H. Horne, J. A. Heraud, and Westland Marston ; but I think there were included many young men, with more aspiration than power, and who, with the egotism of youth, thought in their hearts that they

were the levers destined to move the world.   I
believe I was not the only person who nicknamed the
syncretics the "Mutual Admiration Society." To out-
siders they seemed sadly inarticulate in their teachings,
deficient in that clearness of expression and directness
of aim which usually characterize deep thinkers.

England has often shown a curious way of reward-
ing her men of genius. R. H. Horne must have
been busy in many directions for several years ; we
know he wrote a tragedy or two, and no doubt he was
a journalist, but after the gold discoveries in Australia
he accepted employment as conductor of the escort
which had charge of the treasure. When he returned
to England a circumstance led to the renewal of our
acquaintance, and some time in the " seventies " he
visited us two or three times at Blackheath, in
a quiet sociable way. When I first met him he
was, as I have already said, in the prime of life.
He was about the middle height, and rather portly,
with regular features, eyes that twinkled, and thin
golden-brown hair which arranged itself into little
corkscrew curls. But five and thirty years had of
course worked great changes, for he was now quite
the old man ; his gait was shuffling, and though his
eyes still twinkled, they had lost something of their
fire. He spoke a little of his Australian experiences,
especially of his sufferings from the intense cold at
times, when he had to sleep in the open air, and
when he should have been frozen but for a hot brick

at his feet, the brick having been heated in some primitive manner, which he described, a fire in the earth being made for the purpose. The life he led for so long a time was necessarily one of vigilance—the life, of all others, most opposed to the tranquil rest so conducive to poetical development. He grew more and more infirm, dying at an advanced age, but enjoying a Government pension at the last.

The following letter from R. H. Horne may be left to explain itself. Alas, notwithstanding ten editions of " Orion," the work has not yet reached the general public !

" 7, Northumberland Street, York Gate,
"Regent's Park, W., June 23rd, 1877.

"DEAR MRS. CROSLAND AND MR. CROSLAND,

" I will come next Saturday (the 30th) with much pleasure by five o'clock, or earlier, as the trains decide. But will you kindly send me a post-card as to the train I should take, if the hours differ from the card you previously forwarded ? By *that* card I should take the train at 4.18, so as to arrive at Blackheath at 4.40.

"Respecting the editions of 'Orion,' will you and Mr. Crosland tell me (after due consideration) how many hundreds (or thousands) of pounds are required in *advertising*, in order to enable, not merely the public, but the best people in literature, to hear of a new publication ? You ask me if there are any editions of 'Orion' in a larger type than those first published—*i.e.* any edition since 1843, 1844, or whenever it first appeared. You will both be glad to hear that the poem is now in its tenth edition. There was an edition printed, too, in Australia, besides many in America; but I do not count those, as I am ignorant of the number. Since my return to England —and this is the case for the plaintiff—Ellis and Green published the first library edition in 1872, Chatto and Windus another library edition, viz. the tenth, this in 1874, 1875. This last is nearly exhausted, and I suppose there will be a new edition when the war is over. Meantime, you are not the only persons by several, and all well up in literary matters, who have asked me the very same question. I wish I had a copy to send you. I forget if I sent you a copy of 'Cosmo and other Poems;' if I did not, please let me know, and I will put one in my pocket next Saturday, so that if I am stopped by highwaymen on Blackheath, I shall say, 'There, take that. It is by far the best property I possess.' In which case I shall send you another.

"I remain, dear Mrs. Crosland, most truly,

"R. H. HORNE."

J. A. Heraud was a totally different man from him I have just briefly described, though I suppose he, too, must be considered a poet; at all events he considered himself one of a high order. When I first knew him, early in the "forties," he was the editor of the *Monthly Magazine*, an old-established publication, which, however, was beginning to languish, and, a few years later, died out. He had published one or two long poems, and written several plays, but I do not think they were widely known, or at all remunerative to him. Undoubtedly he was a man of culture and great literary ability, a linguist also, I believe. At any rate, he used to speak as if the acquirement of a language were a matter of only a few weeks. He scarcely, I think, deserved to be called a genius, though he had his flashes of inspiration; witness a sentence which must have been the outcome of bitter disappointment, "We had not to learn that Parnassus is rather a Gethsemane than a Paradise."

Mr. Heraud was a fine critic, and, during his brief editorship of *Fraser's Magazine*, was the happy medium of introducing Carlyle's "Sartor Resartus" to the world. Some years after I first knew him, he was placed on the staff of a very influential journal, where his appreciative and judicial faculties must have had full play, and where he may be said to have "fallen on his feet." But in the early "forties," I think he was chiefly engaged in endeavours to obtain recognition for his own works. He was a married man, with several children, varying downwards, from a son who at this time was in the last stage of a lingering illness, and died before he was eighteen; not, however, until he had shown great promise of literary attainment, writing under the *nom de plume* of Selwyn Cosway. The family lived in Burton Street, Burton Crescent; but it was in one respect a painful home to contemplate, the struggle with poverty was so apparent. Mrs. Heraud must once have been a pretty woman, for, notwithstanding her trying life, she was still comely. I should say she was fairly well educated, but for many years had had no time for reading, consequently she had become something of a human parrot, repeating the praise and censure of things literary which she heard around her. I believe she was a thoroughly good woman, fulfilling many distasteful duties in a really heroic manner. Her hands were hardened by toil, and she had that look of "heart hunger" in her face, which I have noticed more than once in the wives of unsuccessful men—the hunger for rest and peace, and freedom from anxiety, and for a little of the innocent pleasures of life, which are true restoratives. She died in middle age, as such women often do.

John Abraham Heraud was a kindly natured man but, certainly, the greatest egotist I ever knew. He liked very much to read his productions, or selections from them, to admiring friends; and on one occasion it had been arranged that my mother and I were to go to Burton Street on an appointed evening, to hear a play of his read. I believe two or three other friends were expected, but they did not arrive. Not to disappoint us, the dramatist seated

himself at his parlour table, and opened his bulky
quarto manuscript, the only auditors besides ourselves
being his two little girls, who were seated close
together, cosily enjoying the fire. These children
were apparently from eight to ten years old, there
being but little difference in their ages ; one of them
died young, the other grew up to be the actress, Miss
Edith Heraud, but whose health speedily broke down
under the toil and excitement of her profession.
I heard, years afterwards, that this daughter was
stimulated to go on the stage by a strong desire to
appear in her father's plays, and bring them into
notice. I should think, from the little I saw of their
domestic life, that Mr. Heraud had contrived amid
all his cares, to win the hearts of his children.

I have very little recollection of Mrs. Heraud that
evening, for she must have been a good deal out
of the room. I suppose I ought to be ashamed
to own that I utterly forget what the tragedy to
which we listened was about, or even its name—but
one does forget a good many things in the course of
fifty years ! And yet I do distinctly remember the
scene of that parlour. There was very little in-
terruption of the reading ; but once my mother
made some observation, upon which one of the
little girls gleefully exclaimed, " I told you so—
I told you so," but with the half-lisping, half-guttural
articulation of a child who had not been taught to
speak or read well. Evidently the little daughters

were familiar with the play, and listened the more attentively on this account ; for children always enjoy a thrice-told tale more than a novelty, finding great pleasure in watching for what they know is coming. Woe to the *raconteur* who varies his narrative before children.   He is sure to be detected.

I do not recollect what the point was that was briefly discussed at the moment, I only know that the author held to his own opinion.

The reading must have lasted an hour and a half ; at its close, without waiting for comments, the dramatist exclaimed, as he pushed the manuscript a little away—

"It's as fine as anything that ever was written— it's equal to *Macbeth !*"

Such words seemed a thunder-clap—what could one say after them ! Of course we thanked him for the privilege of hearing such a work, with hopes that he would find fit actors to represent the characters. I am sure both my mother and myself felt too much for the man to give him pain by word or look.   It was for others, and for inevitable circumstances, to afford him a more just estimate of his own powers— that is, if anything could do so.

I am afraid the family must have seen many vicis- situdes.   When the head of it was past work, it was understood that the proprietors of the influential journal for which he had long written, allowed him an annuity ; but the invalid daughter was a great

care to him. He ended his days as a brother of the
Charter House, where, in his extreme old age, my
husband visited him, finding him still interested in
literary affairs and in the welfare of his old friends.

It was in the summer of 1842 that I first knew
Westland Marston and his excellent wife. He was a
very young man, not yet three and twenty, to be a
husband and father, and the author of a successful
tragedy which had been the town's talk. But he
bore his honours very becomingly, and all the more
easily because he looked older than his years. I am
not sure, however, that it is good for an author to
have great literary success very early, for, whatever
the merit of his work, it is looked on by one section
of critics in the nature of a promise of still finer
things, and by more ardent admirers as a standard of
excellence by which all future productions must be
measured. If the author himself happens to be well
satisfied with his early work, his wings are a little
clipped for future soaring. This, however, was by no
means the case with Westland Marston, who was
always aspiring, and whose motto might have been
" Excelsior."

Undoubtedly *The Patrician's Daughter* deserved
its success, supported as it was by Macready's personation of the hero, while Helen Faucit increased, if
increase she could, her hold upon the public by her
personation of the " Lady Mabel." This tragedy gave

Westland Marston lasting reputation, for, as "author of the *Patrician's Daughter,*" he was known to the last.   And yet most careful readers would pronounce his later plays more masterly productions.   His prose writings, too, were also admirable.

In the "forties," which was the period in which I saw the most of them, the Marstons' home was a delightful house at which to visit, so many literary, artistic, and the best order of theatrical people being generally their guests.   Mrs. Marston was an admirable woman, a few years older than her husband, and the very wife for him, for she thought a poet was the greatest of God's creations, whom it was a privilege to help and obey.   There was a widespread notion that she was one of the Irish Bourkes ; not so, it was her sister who married a Mr. Bourke, and gave the second name to the poor blind son.   Mrs. Marston's maiden name was Eleanor Potts ; she belonged to a good family, and had a moderate fortune.   I speak with authority, for my husband, one of Marston's oldest friends, was at their wedding, as they were at ours, we having originally met at their house.   Mrs. Marston was a well-informed woman, but without any pretension to literary talent, though a keen appreciator of it ; and she was musical, being a very good pianist.   She, however, neglected music of later years, for her husband, like two or three other poets I have known, was indifferent to the syren voice of the youngest of the Arts.

They lost one little girl in her early childhood, but Mrs. Marston was spared the anguish her husband had to endure, that of surviving their three other children. Yet I think the sorrow of their lives must have been the blindness of their only son, Philip Bourke Marston, who lost his sight when about two years old. He was named after Philip James Bailey, who was one of his sponsors, another being Dinah Mulock, subsequently the author of " John Halifax." When one reflects on what the young poet achieved, with the world-darkness around him, the imagination flags in considering what he might have been under happier circumstances.

Perhaps the pathetic interest excited by the affliction of the son has rendered his productions more widely known to the present generation than the grander, more soul-searching poems of his father, but these can never be allowed to sink utterly into oblivion. The fact is that English poetry is so rich a mine that no individual reader can exhaust it. Lovers of poetry will always have their favourites, and it is infinitely better to know half a dozen great authors well than to skim over the pages of a hundred. Perhaps the time will come when only the few greatest poets will be studied in the completeness of their massive grandeur, while of the somewhat lesser ones we shall merely have selected beauties, the

> " . . . jewels five-words-long
> That on the stretched forefinger of all time
> Sparkle for ever."

U

Plenty of such jewels are there to be found in Horne's "Orion," and Marston's "Gerald and other Poems." Possibly, when the day for making selections arrives, treasures, still longer half-buried, will be brought before the eyes of a rising generation. How few young people of to-day know anything of Goldsmith's "Deserted Village," or Johnson's "Vanity of Human Wishes"! Even Pope is a little shelved!

Yet while I am writing these concluding lines there is abundant evidence that England, from the throned lady of the land to the humblest reader of the Laureate's simplest verses, knows how to honour her great teachers ; for Tennyson lies in his shroud, while the great grave of our "mighty dead" is being prepared to receive his mortal remains. He wrote of one he loved and honoured as enduring without reproach

> ". . . that fierce light which beats upon a throne,
> And blackens every blot."

A "fierce light" also beats on the brow of acknowledged genius, and for fifty out of his eighty-three years he also knew it, without there appearing a blot to blacken.

With Lord Tennyson's death a great epoch seems to have been completed, and with it I will say farewell to such kindly readers as may have followed me in my "Landmarks."

INDEX.

———◦—◦———

A

Aguilar, Grace, descended from a great Jewish family of that name, 171 ; authoress of some interesting and memorable works, 174 ; her elevated character and rare attainments, 174–178 ; her noble and benevolent disposition, 174, 175 ; her "Exposition of Zanoni" attracted the attention and warm commendation of Lord Lytton, then Sir E. Bulwer, 176 ; her death at the early age of thirty-one, 171

Akers, Paul, the American sculptor, the genius shown in his works, 274, 275

Alexis, the clairvoyant, 179 ; the remarkable phenomena he exhibited, 180–183

Annuals, the, *Keepsake* and *Friendship's Offering*, etc., the eminence of the original contributors, the causes of their decline and discontinuance, 95–97

Ansted, Professor and Mrs., visit to, 256

Art Journal, the, its high and beneficial influence, 131

B

Bailey, P. J., the author of "Festus," 212

Barnard, Mrs., her life-like portrait of Mr. S. C. Hall, 125

Beaconsfield, Viscountess, anecdote of her, 103

Beilew, Captain, author of "Memoirs of a Griffin," cured of hydrophobia by an Indian native, 169

Bernard, Bayle, dramatist and journalist ; the principal characters in some of his plays acted by Tryone Power, 169

Birmingham riots, the, anecdotes of, 11, 12

Black Dwarf, the ; visit to his hovel, 77

Blanc, Louis, description of his person and manners, 189

Blessington, Lady ; her home, Gore House, described ; her talents, manners, history, mode of life, and appearance, 97–113, 117 ; her superb sapphire ring, 114 ; her death, 118

Bonheur, Rosa, her handsome face and masculine qualities, 138 ;

of Lady Blessington and contributor to the *Keepsake*, 100,
101
Clerk of the Kitchen " to George
IV., Monsieur V——, 37
Cowden Clarke, Mrs., compiler of
the "Concordance of Shakespeare"; her admirable acting of
"Mrs. Malaprop," 187; her "Girlhood of Shakespeare's Heroines,"
a work of great merit and interest,
188
Craik, Mrs. *See* Mulock, Miss
Crowe, Mrs., 86
Cushman, Charlotte, a woman of
genius and a great actress, 206–
208; her power and skill as a
dramatic reader, 208

D

D'Angoulême, Duchess, her mourn-
ful appearance, 28
Davison, Mrs., the actress; her
performance of "Lady Teazle"
and other parts, 43–46
Davison, James, her son, who became the musical critic of the
Times newspaper; his boyhood,
44
"Delta" of *Blackwood's Magazine*,
D. M. Moir, 86
D'Orsay, Count, 110–112; description of him, his residence, his
relations with Lady Blessington,
113–116
Drummond, Myra, the artist, paints
a remarkably effective portrait of
Helen Faucit, 200; employs a
soldier as a model and afterwards
marries him, 202–204; her pride
and poverty, 204, 205

E

Emigrès, French. *See* French
Emigrès

F

Farren, Miss, the actress, who
became Lady Derby, prophesying
that Mrs. Davison would be her
successor, 46
Faucit, Helen (Lady Martin), a
remarkable portrait of her painted
by Myra Drummond; her celebrity as an actress, 200, 201
Fields, J. T., of Boston, U.S.A.
See Ticknor and Fields
French Emigrès, the family of the
Gautherots described; the middle-
class society of the period and the
fashions of the time which prevailed, 17–23
Fuller, Margaret, the celebrated
American authoress; her talents,
characteristics, and career, 223–
225; marries the Marchese Ossoli,
225; drowned, 226

G

George III. at the theatre, 14;
Queen Charlotte's snuff-taking,
14; death of the king, his life
and character commended, 29
George IV., incidents of his coronation described, 33; meeting
his discarded wife at the theatre,
36; partaking of a steak in the
kitchen with some convivial companions, 37
Gibson the sculptor; his tinted
Venus, 273

THE END.

LONDON : PRINTED BY WILLIAM CLOWES AND SONS, LIMITED,
STAMFORD STREET AND CHARING CROSS.

For EU product safety concerns, contact us at Calle de José Abascal, 56–1°, 28003 Madrid, Spain or eugpsr@cambridge.org.

www.ingramcontent.com/pod-product-compliance
Ingram Content Group UK Ltd.
Pitfield, Milton Keynes, MK11 3LW, UK
UKHW010349140625
459647UK00010B/933